CARMELITE BIOGRAI

CW00457519

A STUMBLING PILGRIM GUIDED BY INDIRECTIONS

A biography of Carmelite friar Fr. Malachy Lynch (1899-1972)

BY WILFRID MCGREAL, O.CARM.

Saint Albert's Press
2016

Photography: Mr. Johan Bergström-Allen, T.O.C.; Mr. Charles Bodiam; Mr. Roger Brown; Fr. Richard Copsey, O.Carm.; Fox Photos; Jarrolds; Kent Messenger (The County Paper of Kent); Keystone Press Agency; Mr. J. S. Markiewicz; Thomas Neile Ltd., Whiststable; Skyscan Balloon Photography, Cheltenham; Sport and General Press Agency; Topham Picturepoint.

Frontispiece sketch of Fr. Malachy and Aylesford Priory reproduced from *The Desert Shall Bloom* by kind permission of the Superior and Community of Ware Carmelite Monastery.

The British Province of Carmelites does not necessarily endorse the individual views contained in its publications.

First published 2016 by Saint Albert's Press.

Saint Albert's Press
Whitefriars, 35 Tanners Street,
Faversham, Kent, ME13 7JN, United Kingdom
www.carmelite.org

Book ISBN-10: 0-904849-48-1
Book ISBN-13: 978-0-904849-48-6

ePub ISBN-10: 0-904849-49-X
ePub ISBN-13: 978-0-904849-49-3

Edited and designed by Johan Bergström-Allen, Carmelite Communications & Outreach Office, York.

Typeset and printed by Inc Dot Design & Print, York.

Fr. MALACHY LYNCH

first Prior of the Return.

FOREWORD

It is now some 25 years since I sat down to prepare a new edition of *Courage to Build Anew*, a telling of the historic return of the Carmelite friars to their ancient home at Aylesford Priory, told in the *Pilgrims' Newsletters* of Father Malachy Lynch, O.Carm., as edited by Gabriel Fielding. That we are still telling Malachy's story, 25 years after that publication and more than 40 years since his death in 1972, is a mark of the stature of this man. Malachy was one of three brothers to become friars, sons of the farm in County Wicklow who, each in his own way, had a transformative impact on the Carmelite Order across the world.

In the prologue to his Gospel, Saint Luke says that he has consulted those who were *"from the beginning eyewitnesses"* (*Luke* 1:2). Wilfrid McGreal is perhaps uniquely placed to be such an eyewitness, to tell us of the man behind the *Pilgrims' Newsletters* and behind the great work of restoration and renewal of Carmelite life at Aylesford. Importantly, Wilfrid knew not just Malachy the man and the priest-friar as a fellow brother, but essentially knew him within the context of Malachy's family of origin.

The telling of the story has been a labour of love for Wilfrid. Love certainly for Malachy, with all his complexity and genius, but love also for his brothers in gifting to us a part of our story as told by an *eyewitness* who is trustworthy and reliable.

At Malachy's funeral, as the coffin lay in the piazza before the great restored sanctuary below the statue of the Glorious Assumption of Our Lady, the preacher, Fr. Edward Maguire, said these words which are on the gravestone of Sir Christopher Wren, architect of Saint Paul's Cathedral in London: *si monumentum requires circumspice – if you are looking for his monument, look around you.*

6

With his own genius and insight, Wilfrid has given us a new and arguably better monument to this unique Carmelite. Not one made of stone and glass, but one that tells of frail flesh and blood, and humanity placed at the service of God and his Mother. For this we owe Wilfrid a great debt, as will the generations that follow.

Our thanks to Wilfrid, and to all those who have helped in the collecting and ordering of the material. A particular thanks to Malachy's family in Wicklow, and to our brothers in the Irish Province of Carmelites who gave access to their archive; to Johan Bergström-Allen who has edited this text; and to Francis Kemsley who has brought out of the British Province archive images both old and those not seen before.

Very Rev. Fr. Antony Lester, O.Carm.
Prior Provincial of the British Province of Carmelites
16th May 2016 – Feast of St. Simon Stock

7

Dedication

To Jane Deeson, with thanks for your friendship and support

Introduction

The Lynch brothers (l-r): Malachy, Elias, Kilian.

The British Province of Carmelite friars, and perhaps the Church in Britain at large, owes a great deal to three brothers: Elias, Malachy, and Kilian Lynch. Three very different characters, but all gifted with amazing energy and vision. They were in turn pragmatic, poetic, and academic. Elias and Malachy were to leave Ireland and minister in Britain, while Kilian – after years in America and Rome – was to spend his middle years in England supporting Malachy. Each of the brothers had amazing energy; something of the Wicklow Mountains was part of their D.N.A.

I have already told something of Elias' story in *Friar Beyond the Pale*, and now I would like to focus on Malachy's life, celebrating a visionary character and yet, in many ways, vulnerable and in need of support.

I first met Malachy in 1955 when I spent a few days as a volunteer at The Friars, the ancient Carmelite priory in the Kent village of Aylesford. Malachy struck me as a commanding personality; tall with a shock of white hair and strong features, his Carmelite habit added to the presence of the man. Two years later I became a novice friar at Aylesford, and Malachy was Prior of a large and varied community. Malachy was at his peak, and he was an imposing figure with his white cloak flung over the brown habit.

9

We were all, to some degree, in awe of Malachy, and aware that we had become part of a great adventure that was the restoration of Aylesford, reoccupied by the Carmelites in 1949. My most vivid memories are not so much Malachy preaching to great crowds of pilgrims, but the community Chapter meeting where he galvanised us into action. There were 14 novices and we were a mixture of ages and backgrounds. Then there were the (non-ordained) brothers: Brother Michael the potter, and Brother David the printer, and Brother John to name a few. And over and above us were the priests, including Michael Wall the Novice Master, and Brocard Sewell who ran Saint Albert's Press. The community had at its peak the priests, and each group had their own common room. So the Chapter brought all the elements of the community together – priests, brothers, and novices – and gave Malachy a chance to share his vision and his encouragement. He was annoyed if tools were left lying about: he said they should be treated like the chalices used at Mass. Those who found it hard to get up were told to jump out of bed as if it were on fire. However, his main thrust was being involved in the restoration of the priory and never being idle. It was important that the prior should see you engaged usefully.

Malachy Lynch in his Carmelite white cloak.

Despite the hard work there was the sense that you were involved in something significant; we shared in having "courage to build anew", as Malachy put it. We were all aware that Malachy drove himself at a cost as he lived with diabetes, and also could be overwhelmed by the whole project. He had, however, a vision and a dream, which at

10

times was not always grasped by his confreres. One of his aphorisms that summed up his frustration was "the devil of incongruity".

The Father Malachy I knew as a novice had come a long way from his home in County Wicklow, Ireland. Life had shaped him, and friendships had enabled him. He was an obedient friar: taking on the parish at Faversham in Kent when aged only 27; then his commitment as Novice Master, a role he left with sadness to go to Wales in 1936; and finally to take on the task of restoring Aylesford, with some help from Elias his brother and Provincial Bursar, but basically putting out into the deep, into unchartered seas. Above all, Malachy believed in what he was doing and was fortunate in having friends who believed in his vision, one he shared in all 113 editions of the *Pilgrims' Newsletter* sent to friends and supporters of the Carmelites at Aylesford.

I am grateful for help and hospitality from the Carmelite community at Gort Muire in Dublin: Anselm Corbett in reminiscing gives a picture of Malachy as Novice Master, while correspondence in the archives at Gort Muire gives background to the time at Aberystwyth. I have quarried the newsletters which are a rich seam of inspiration, and for the last five years of Malachy's life we were members of the Aylesford community, though living at Allington Castle.

I hope what follows gives a sense of the man, and hoping to keep his memory alive. I am conscious that what follows is very much a sketch, but it also says something about Catholicism in the middle of the 20th Century.

Very Rev. Fr. Wilfrid McGreal, O.Carm.
Prior of Faversham
8th January 2016 – Feast of Saint Peter Thomas

11

Malachy Lynch

The Carmelite Order owes a debt of gratitude to the Lynch family, and especially the three younger brothers of a family of thirteen. The Lynches farmed land in County Wicklow at Ballymanus near Aughram. They had originally come from Carlow to Ballymanus in the mid-19th Century. The names of these brothers were Murtha, William, and Edward, but better known as Carmelites by their religious names: Elias, Malachy, and Kilian. William, the subject of this biography, was born on 31st July 1899.

Ballymanus, the Lynch family home in County Wicklow.

St. Brigid's Church in Annacurra, County Wicklow, where the Lynch family worshipped.

12

The boys' father was a person of dignity and integrity, involved also in the life of the local community. He was a fine role model, and in all he did he was supported by his wife who had the task of caring for a large household with so many mouths to feed. She could be quite fierce, but she cared tenderly for the family and she always had food for any man on the road. Her children remembered her apple pies and the warmth of the kitchen, a welcome oasis in a big and draughty house.

Dublin in the early 20ᵗʰ Century.

Tragedy visited the family when – the eldest of the three boys being just twelve – their father died aged barely fifty. This meant radical changes as the breadwinner was gone. Fortunately, the elder children were able to keep the farm going while others went to work in Dublin. Elias, the eldest of the three, got an office job in Dublin, while Malachy and Kilian continued at the National School, finishing their basic education.

Early days

By a series of adventures Elias was accepted as a postulant by the Carmelite friars, and joined the community at Terenure College in Dublin. Elias, in a spirit of schoolboy romance, had been attracted to the British Army, but fortunately the call of a religious vocation prevailed. Thousands of young Irishmen did join the British Army and were to die in the Somme.

The other brothers, Malachy and Kilian, followed Elias into the Carmelite novitiate and a time of study so they could matriculate and qualify for university entrance.

13

Terenure College, Dublin.

The Carmelites and students at Terenure College, Autumn 1914.

14

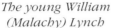

*The young William
(Malachy) Lynch*

*Fr. Peter Elias Magennis,
O.Carm., Prior General*

The struggle for independence from Britain made life difficult in Ireland, and by 1920 the student friars were dispatched to Rome where the Prior General, Elias Magennis, organised accommodation for this group of young Irish friars.

Finding a place for the students was not easy, as a great deal of Church property had been sequestrated by the Italian State. The Carmelites were able to rent their priory of San Martino ai Monti which is near Santa Maria Maggiore. It was somewhere to live but was far from homely. (Today San Martino belongs again to the Order and is a lively parish and centre for student friars.)

*The basilica and parish of San Martino ai Monti in Rome
was first entrusted to the Carmelites in the 13th Century.*

15

Father Elias Lynch has vivid memories of his time in Rome, signalling colourful characters and telling whimsical tales; to him the whole event was an adventure. Malachy, on the other hand, found the experience less than exciting. He was plagued by ill health, and really glad after ordination in 1925 to leave Rome and begin pastoral work with young people in Dublin, based in Whitefriar Street, a busy city-centre church. Elias also came back to Dublin, but Kilian was recognised as an academic and would stay on working for a doctorate.

Whitefriars Street Church, Dublin. The Carmelites have had a presence in Ireland since 1279, and in Dublin soon after. The present church building, consecrated in 1827, stands on the site of the pre-Reformation priory.

Malachy Lynch as a young Carmelite.

Parish Priest at Faversham

Malachy didn't realise that he had come back to Ireland at a time when momentous decisions were being taken in the Carmelite Order that would change his life. The Prior Provincial of the Irish Carmelites, John Cogan, encouraged by the Prior General Elias Magennis, was trying to get a foothold in the English county of Kent so that sometime in the future there might be a chance of regaining Aylesford Priory.

16

Aylesford was regarded as a site of special historical and spiritual significance for the Carmelite Order. It had been founded as a hermitage in 1242 by hermits from Mount Carmel in the Holy Land, the Order's place of origin. The first General Chapter of the hermits took place at Aylesford in 1247, at which they took momentous decisions that would lead to the Carmelites becoming an order of mendicant friars (begging brothers). In the late Middle Ages the priory at Aylesford grew as a centre of hospitality for pilgrims en route to the shrine of St. Thomas Becket at Canterbury. Being associated with Saint Simon Stock, an early Prior General of the Carmelites renowned for his holiness, Aylesford

Fr. John Cogan.

came to be seen as a holy site in its own right. However, with the Reformation of the Church in England, King Henry VIII dissolved religious communities, and in 1538 the priory was taken from the Carmelites and given into private hands. The site retained many of the beautiful medieval priory buildings, under the name of "The Friars". Because of its importance in the Carmelites' sense of history and identity, members of the Order worldwide were keen to see a community of friars restored at Aylesford one day.

The expulsion of the Carmelites from Aylesford depicted at The Friars in a painting by Adam Kossowski.

17

An anonymous painting of The Friars in the early 17th Century,
at Packington Hall, Warwickshire, seat of the Earl of Aylesford.

Accordingly, with an eye on eventually returning to Aylesford, the Carmelite Order agreed in 1926 to take on the pastoral care of Catholic parishes in Faversham and Sittingbourne, two neighbouring towns in Kent. Sittingbourne held some promise, but Faversham held very little in the way of potential. Malachy was not happy to be asked to go to Kent with John Cogan and become Parish Priest of Faversham. Faversham was a challenge, with its ramshackle house and tiny chapel tucked away in Plantation Road. The house and chapel dated from the early years of the 20th Century. Malachy was young to be

Interior of the Catholic Church of Our Lady of Compassion and St. Theodore on Plantation Road, Faversham, established 1899. The name changed to Our Lady of Mount Carmel when the Church and Carmelite Friary moved to Tanners Street in 1937.

18

given care of a parish (he was just twenty-seven), a fine, tall, strong-featured young friar with plenty of energy. The parishioners were intrigued at having such a young pastor, and wondered if he had been sent to Faversham because of some misdemeanour.

Coming to minister in Kent was also a culture shock as Catholics were very much in a minority, and the few Catholics that were in the town were rather looked down upon. Malachy felt there was an anti-Catholic atmosphere, and the prevailing ethos was dull and respectable – a far cry from Dublin and Rome. However, Malachy was not daunted and began to explore the parish which covered the town and surrounding villages. Cycling round the villages he discovered lots of Catholics hidden away. Being young himself he was able to be accepted by the young parishioners, and organised events to encourage their faith. In 1929 he organised a Mass in the ruins of Faversham Abbey to celebrate the centenary of Catholic Emancipation in Britain.

Fr. Malachy celebrating Mass in the ruins of Faversham Abbey.

Life was austere with little money for any luxuries, and a leg of lamb had to do for the whole week, roasted or cold cuts. In his ministry Malachy was helped by Brother Franco, a Maltese friar, and Fr. Cogan in Sittingbourne was always helpful. To give each other support and for company they would get the bus to Teynham which

19

is halfway between Faversham and Sittingbourne on the old Roman road. Perhaps they chatted away over a pint and a sandwich in the old Dover Castle coaching inn.

Dover Castle Inn, Teynham.

Novice Master

Malachy was not meant to stay in Faversham, as in 1930 he was appointed Master of Novices. He had come to like his ministry in Faversham, and especially the outreach in the villages all endowed with beautiful medieval churches, a reminder of a time before the Reformation. However, he was not to know that he would return to Kent when the most significant time of his life would bring him to Aylesford and its restoration; but that was waiting twenty years in the future. Nor would anyone have dreamt that Malachy's elder brother Elias would come to Faversham and transform the parish, and – through establishing the National Shrine of Saint Jude – make it known far and wide.

Kinsale in County Cork was a novitiate for the Irish Province. There had been a Carmelite Priory from the Middle Ages, and a new church and priory were built in the 19th Century. The priory was built on a hillside overlooking the town and the harbour. Kinsale was a British garrison town, and after the Irish War of Independence (1919-21) many former soldiers stayed on, marrying local women and becoming Catholics.

20

Kinsale Harbour. The Carmelite Friary and its Church can be seen top right.

Interior of the Carmelite Friary Church in Kinsale.

21

Kinsale, set in such natural beauty, was an ideal place for a Carmelite novitiate. It was also to prove a creative context for Malachy. During his residence in Kent he had found time to explore the beauty of the cathedrals with their stained glass and fine carvings. All of this began to awake in Malachy his aesthetic sense, a love of beauty and craftsmanship. He also encouraged the novice friars to appreciate beauty in art and nature. He saw love, art, music and an ability to ensure its place in worship, as important features of their formation. One of his novices, Anselm Corbett, remembers their music teacher: a former military bandmaster whom Malachy conscripted to help the novice team to read music. Malachy encouraged the novices to explore the countryside and to enjoy swimming in the Atlantic. The impression we get of Malachy as a novice master was a desire to help the whole person grow, and not to be caught up in minutiae: the novices needed to be helped to grow and flourish. Malachy found friendships with the local clergy helped him open up to the aesthetic, and grow in appreciation of the world of art and literature. Reflecting back on his time in Kinsale, Malachy wrote:

> In Kinsale most of the people were Catholic and almost half-mystical. Fr. McSwiney who was on the staff of the Parish Church and Professor Fleischman became my great friends. They were certainly international in their interests and were very cultured people. A walk which we planned once a week was really a great occasion for learning about many things ... There was also a Jesuit priest who was a scholar and living with his people locally at the time. He used to carry a glass in his pocket and sample all the wells within walking distance of the town. He was a

22

shy man and was compiling an Irish dictionary. From the point of view of meeting people of like interest it was an ideal situation. I shall always be under a debt of gratitude to the ordinary people of the neighbourhood who were most loving and helpful in every way. I felt that with them I knew Ireland for the first time and appreciated it more than I can say. Although seemingly cut off, it was the richest period in my life and it certainly looks like a paradox. Now I know what the Faith means when it is really deep and loved by those who have it. It is not just the catechism but it is made of all the generations that have gone before.

1971 Bulletin of the England and Wales Carmelite Province

During Malchy's time in Kinsale, the Prior General of the Order called all the novice masters for a meeting in Rome. An outcome of the meeting was the *Carmelite Directory of the Spiritual Life* which was to be an important aid in the formation of novices. Another outcome of the conference was a visit to Ireland in 1935 by Titus Brandsma. Titus was a Dutch Carmelite friar, professor at Nijmegen University, and an insightful lecturer on the great Carmelite mystics. He was an outspoken critic of the Nazis, and was to perish as a martyr in Dachau in 1942. This short encounter with Titus must have influenced Malachy. Titus was a scholar, a person of prayer, and courageously outspoken in defence of the Gospel against the Nazi ideology.

23

Painting of Titus Brandsma by Collette Mills at Kinsale Carmelite Friary.

In 1935 Malachy's mother died. She had been a woman of energy, determination and prayer. When her husband had died suddenly while still young she had had to shoulder responsibility for a large family. Malachy and Elias were able to be with their mother at the end, saying Mass in the house at Ballymanus, bringing a prayerful woman the support of prayer at her passing.

Malachy's time in Kinsale was soon to end, but he had found the years he spent there life-enhancing. Through the friends he made he gained great experiences on the cultural and spiritual level; he felt it was the richest period of his life and gave him resources that would stand him in good stead for the rest.

Malachy (middle row, left-hand side) with fellow Carmelites at a jubilee celebration in Kinsale, 1948.

24

Called to minister in Wales

In 1936 Malachy found himself called to minister in Wales. Father Cogan, the Provincial, was a friend of Dr. Michael McGrath, Bishop of Menevia. The Carmelites were invited to take on the pastoral care of the parish of Our Lady of the Angels and St. Winefride at Aberystwyth, and were asked to re-establish the junior seminary in the town, St. Mary's College. The College was almost derelict, so no small effort was needed to repair the building, and also to recruit possible young people who felt called to the priesthood. Besides the College there was the question of the parish which covered the best part of the county of Cardiganshire. Aberystwyth was also a university town which meant additional care would be needed for the student population.

(L) St. Mary's College, Aberystwyth, now the Welsh Book Council.
(R) Catholic Church of Our Lady of the Angels & St. Winefride.

The task was daunting, with only a handful of friars to provide pastoral care. Besides Malachy, there were two young friars – Michael (known as Pop) Kiely and Patrick Geary – both of whom were to spend many years ministering in Wales.

Left: The young Fr. Patrick Geary. Right: Fr. Michael Kiely with the author in 1977.

25

Getting the College ready and settling into the parish proved exacting tasks, and besides all that was happening at Aberystwyth there was pressure from the bishop to develop pastoral care for Lampeter, a town some 30 miles to the southeast. Malachy found the demands being made on the community quite exhausting. It was decided to appoint Fr. Bonaventure Fitzgerald as Parish Priest. Bonaventure had only recently been ordained, but what he lacked in experience he made up for in enthusiasm. He was later to become Parish Priest in Sittingbourne, and was Prior Provincial in the 1950s. While he was in Aberystwyth he gave special attention to parish visitations, seeking out the sick and elderly.

Lampeter

With St. Mary's College up and running, Malachy focussed his attention on developing 'Whitefriars' at Lampeter. He had the support of the Wynnes, a prominent Catholic family in the area, and the Old Barn at their estate in Garthewine was the inspiration for the Catholic church at Lampeter. The architect, Thomas H. B. Scott, incorporated features of the barn into the design of the new church and was generous with his time and expertise. It seems that he was a Carmelite Tertiary (a professed lay member of the Order) and was happy to be of service.

 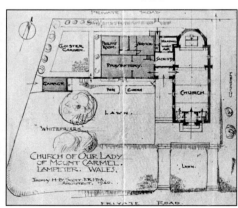

Left: The interior of Our Lady of Mount Carmel Church, Lampeter, as designed by Thomas Scott.

Right: Thomas Scott's plan of 'Whitefriars', Lampeter, as shown on appeal literature in 1940.

26

The church was dedicated by Dr. McGrath on the feast of Our Lady of Mount Carmel, 16th July 1940 – just in time as wartime building regulations were just coming into force. Malachy was successful in raising the £5,000 needed for the project, the money coming from Dublin schoolchildren among others. To begin with there was no resident priest, so Mrs. Wynne lived in the presbytery caring for the church. The arrival of evacuees saw the necessity of a resident priest.

Corpus Christi procession in the grounds of the Catholic Church in Lampeter.

Malachy saw that the furnishings of the church were in good taste. Writing in 1971, he reminisced about the decoration: *"Artists turned up and gave their services. Everything was made by hand and local workers were proud that their skill was used by the Church."* Malachy went on to describe how the Sisters of Charity made the vestments, and Dunstan Prudens from the Ditchling community crafted the sacred vessels, while the furnishing of the church was the work of a Czech craftsman, Jaroslav Kreshler, who also carved the Stations of the Cross. Malachy was surprised at the low cost of the whole enterprise and the efficiency of the contractor.

The Carmelites cared for Lampeter until 1970. Father Gregory FitzGerald, during his time in Lampeter, was chosen as Mayor in recognition of his work for the whole community.

Difficult days

Returning to Aberystwyth, Malachy became an officiating chaplain to the Royal Air Force, and was also chaplain to the Catholic community at the University. Aberystwyth was transformed from a quiet holiday town by the war, with the arrival of evacuees from London and the presence of the military. The University took in evacuees and with all this influx the Catholic church became a busy place. The whole Carmelite community was busy indeed. Mass centres were

27

established throughout most of Cardiganshire, which meant that the Carmelites would have to travel miles enabling the Eucharist to be celebrated. At this time there was a strict Eucharistic fast, so that the priest would only eat when he returned to Aberystwyth.

The Church of Our Lady of Mount Carmel, Lampeter, today.

On top of the immense amount of pastoral work the community had the responsibility of St. Mary's College and its students. The constant refrain in correspondence and meetings was that the buildings were inadequate, there were too few friars to teach the students, and finance would make it difficult to employ lay teachers. Father Malachy had to care for the community, give time to teaching, and carry out the ever-increasing pastoral demands. A number of future Carmelite friars studied at the College, including Edward Maguire, and the brothers John and Gregory FitzGerald. The FitzGerald brothers were to play a significant part in the life of the Order and the Catholic Church in Wales. Malachy was ably supported during this difficult time by Patrick Geary who was indefatigable in his commitment. He was later to be Provincial Superior of the Order.

Fr. John FitzGerald was a major figure in the development of Catholic culture in Wales.

It soon became clear that with new educational legislation coming in the College at Aberystwyth could never meet the new demands. A property was needed that could accommodate an appropriate range of academic subjects, and there was also a need for sports facilities. A search for properties that would be suitable was prolonged and frustrating. Father Elias Lynch gave all the support that was possible, but the Carmelite community in

28

Aberystwyth felt isolated. There was also the perception that the Carmelite Provincial and Council in Dublin lacked an awareness of the pressure that the friars in Wales were experiencing. Malachy had the task of trying to negotiate with Dublin, and also keep the Welsh Catholic bishops aware that the Carmelites were committed to education. Doctor McGrath – appointed Archbishop of Cardiff in 1940 – was fully aware of these difficulties as he had been the Rector of the College in the 1930s

A letter from the Carmelite community in 1944 catalogues the inadequacies of the building, with no recreational or medical facilities. During a flu epidemic there was no space for those who were really ill. In one case a friar gave up his room for a sick boy and slept in the utility room. It was estimated that £50,000 would be needed to bring everything to a reasonable state – that was a considerable sum for the 1940s. In writing this letter Malachy had the support of the whole community.

In January 1944 Malachy wrote an angry letter to the Carmelite Provincial in Dublin, complaining that money meant for Aberystwyth was being used to build-up a fund for the new Irish house of studies. Malachy was plainly aggrieved, and felt that his brother Elias had colluded in this use of the monies. Malachy and Elias often clashed over finance, but in reality Elias often felt that his younger brother could be disingenuous. It is interesting to note that if an outsider criticised one or other of the Lynches, the brothers would always close ranks and spare no quarter. In these letters there is also a concern for the quality of community life in England and Wales, and a reminder that the Order was respected.

The fact that the Aberystwyth community and its prior felt badly done by can be seen in a note to the Provincial, James O'Shea, written by the Secretary to the House Chapter, Dominic Reale. Dominic Reale enclosed the prior's letter and wrote: *"the Community are convinced of the justice of their case and they are demonstrating justice"*; fighting talk in an era where usually friars would be loath to give such strong expression of their feelings to superiors.

29

The move to Llandeilo

It was accepted that St. Mary's College at Aberystwyth could never provide educational facilities for all needs, and so from 1945 onwards a search began for a more suitable property. After a series of false starts, a property was found some seventy miles to the southeast in Llandeilo. Tregyb, as it was called, was a fine château-styled building set in some 100 acres of farm and woodland. The property was bought from a Baroness Rutzen who, despite her name, was English. The purchase and setting-up of the property as a school fell on the shoulders of Malachy and Pat Geary. The finance was forthcoming through the efforts of Malachy's brother Elias, who engaged in some focussed fundraising. The cost of purchase and setting-up came to £30,000. Malachy was enthusiastic about the project and pleased that Tregyb had good transport links.

For Malachy there was some sadness in moving from Aberystwyth, with memories of days when hospitality was offered to distinguished guests who sought safety in Wales. One person who delighted Malachy was Saunders Lewis, a great Welsh nationalist and literary figure. Saunders was out of favour with the authorities, and Malachy gave him a post as a teacher when otherwise employment would have been out of the question. Saunders taught Welsh and was a leading Welsh dramatist and poet. Malachy admired his literary gifts and the fervour of his newly found Catholic faith. Malachy's delight in his company and literary talents caused him to compare Saunders Lewis to the French diplomat and poet Paul Claudel, another devout Catholic.

Tregyb, Llandeilo.

30

Once Tregyb was purchased in late 1946 there was the task of turning the house into a school. Setting up the school was a major operation and not without controversy. Malachy and Elias had fallen out about what furniture should be bought from the previous owner, but in the end peace prevailed. As ever Pat Geary was there to support Malachy, and the new school was opened on

Saunders Lewis who, in 1925, had co-founded Plaid Genedlaethol Cymru (the National Party of Wales), later known as Plaid Cyrmu.

24th September 1947 with Mass celebrated by Bishop John Petit of Menevia. The College at Aberystwyth found a new purpose when it became the second centre for training late vocations to the priesthood. The bishop gave this project his blessing and Pat Geary took on the responsibility for the new venture, however, with very little help.

The school at Tregyb was also a Mass centre for Llandeilo, but as it was on the edge of the town there was a need for something more central. More by luck than planning, a property was found in the town. So on the Feast of Saint Teresa, Malachy signed the contract and Cefn Goleu (Ridge of Light) became the parish centre in the town.

About this time Malachy was given six statues for the school chapel, sculpted by Philip Lindsey Clark. Timber was scarce, so wood from an old Thames barge was used. This commission began a relationship with the Clark family that was to be so important in the restoration of Aylesford.

Prior of Aylesford

Malachy was not to spend much time at the new college as in the late 1940s the prospect arose of purchasing The Friars at Aylesford, once among the most significant priories in the Carmelite Order.

Malachy had visited Aylesford in 1929 in the company of the Prior

31

General, Elias Magennis. He remembered the warm welcome they had received from the then owner, Mrs. Woolsey and her son-in-law Mr. Copley de Lisle Hewitt, as a sign of future promise.

Mr. Copley de Lisle Hewitt on his horse Peter by the front door of The Friars.

No doubt Malachy was saddened to hear about a fire in 1930 that caused immense damage to The Friars, but the ensuing restoration work brought to light many original features of the medieval priory.

Care was lavished on The Friars by Mrs. Woolsey and Mr. Hewitt, who restored and developed the buildings in the two decades after the fire. But World War II (1939-45) brought change to all sections of

32

The West Cloister at The Friars after the fire of 1930.

The Friars after the fire of 1930.

society, and towards the end of the 1940s Copley Hewitt's son, Mr. Woolsey Hewitt, expressed a desire to put The Friars on the market. The Carmelites began preparing themselves, seeking aid from various quarters of the Catholic community.

33

The Secretariat of State of His Holiness,
N.186054

The Vatican: 18th September, 1948.

Most Rev. Father,

        The August Pontiff was most pleased to learn from the
recent letter of the Most Rev. Father, that with the consent
of the Curia of the Carmelite Order of the Ancient Observance,
you, the Prior General of that Order, are preparing to
acquire again the Convent of Aylesford - a Convent rich in
memories and associations, and, above all, distinguished for
having sheltered within its walls, Saint Simon Stock.

        Grieving that the burdens which are at present so heavy
on the Holy See, do not allow him to forward the project with
the generosity of a donation of his own, the Holy Father does
not doubt, but that the Divine Providence will provide, in due
time, ways and means for the furthering of an undertaking
from which there is good reason to hope that great spiritual
good will come to your religious family.   Trusting, meanwhile,
that a happy outcome will crown your efforts, the Holy Father
imparts the Apostolic Benediction to you and your brethren, and
to all, who, by their moral or material help, come to your
help in realising such a praiseworthy undertaking.

        With deep feelings of respect,

            I am, Most Rev. Father,

                Yours most Devotedly in Our Lord,

                    (G.B. Montini).

The Most Rev. Father E. Kilian Lynch,
Prior General of the Carmelites of the Old Observance.

*A letter from the Vatican to the Carmelite Prior General, dated September 1948,
shows that the Order sought unsuccessfully to secure financial help from Pope Pius
XII to buy back The Friars.*

In 1949 The Friars was finally put on the market. After negotiations
with the Carmelites the purchase was agreed on 20th June for £25,000.

34

WHITEFRIARS
FAVERSHAM
KENT

20 June 1949

This morning at 12/30 pm, was signed in the presence of the following people, the contract for purchase of the Friars Aylesford. on behalf of the Calced Carmelite.

M. Elias Lynch. O. Carm Faversham

D. H. L. Hardgrove, solicitor, Sittingbourne

P. Edwin Scally; O. Carm. Prior, Faversham

B. L. Rogan O.Carm. prior, Sittingbourne

W. J. Hastings O.Carm. Sittingbourne

P Leo Maher OCarm Lay Brother Sittingbourne
P. Anthony McGreal O. Carm. Lay Brother Faversham

Carmelite Priory

Sittingbourne Kent.

A document listing those Carmelites who witnessed the signing of the contract purchasing The Friars.

35

The Prior General, Kilian Lynch, and his brother Elias were responsible for raising the money and gaining support from all over the Order. This new project was under the jurisdiction of the Prior General, and Fr. Kilian turned to his brother Malachy to take on the role of Prior of Aylesford. This was a daunting task, and one that would become his life's work. Malachy was just fifty years old in 1949, with great experience of enabling projects, and a firm sense of the providence of God. Malachy's time as novice master had deepened his prayer life, and he had a great sense of beauty and order. An inspiring man, he did not enjoy good health and lived with diabetes, but above all he believed in what he was doing and whom he was serving.

Malachy and Kilian taking (back) possession of The Friars in 1949.

The Carmelites processing over Aylesford Bridge.

The return of the Carmelite friars to their old home took place on 31st October 1949, just over four hundred years since the Order had been turned out. Some fifty Whitefriars (so-called because of the Order's white cloak) processed over the medieval bridge in Aylesford, up through the village and through the gatehouse to the old priory.

36

The Whitefriars processing through Aylesford village. The cross is being carried by Brother Anthony McGreal, the author's uncle.

A painting at The Friars by Adam Kossowski depicts the Carmelites returning through the medieval Gatehouse. Malachy is shown leading the group of Whitefriars on the right, with his brother Elias looking up, fifth from the right. Their brother Kilian is shown following the cross-bearer on the left.

37

The medieval refectory was used as the Upper Chapel and served as the priory church until the Main Shrine was built.

The medieval refectory was transformed into an upper chapel, and a great deal had been done to make the place able to accommodate a community.

The initial community was just four friars, but was helped by committed friends, including a group of women who were part of a newly constituted 'secular institute', that is, an organisation of consecrated persons professing the evangelical counsels (chastity, poverty, and obedience) whilst living 'in the world' rather than enclosed in a monastery or nunnery. Fathers Kilian and Malachy were keen that in Britain the Carmelite Family should be built up in all its diversity, recognising that the work of the friars would be greatly enhanced by the prayers and collaboration of a group of lay people.

The founding members of the 'Institute of Our Lady of Mount Carmel' – which would later be known as 'The Leaven' – were among those who witnessed the Whitefriars return to Aylesford on 31st October.

Having processed to their restored home the friars kept vigil, and early on the morning of All Saints Day, Mass was celebrated and the Prior General formally installed Malachy as Prior of Aylesford.

Kilian installs his brother Malachy as Prior of Aylesford in the Upper Chapel.

The return of the Carmelites to their 'old home' touched the imagination of the Catholic community in Britain and Ireland. As well as being the site of the first General Chapter of the Carmelite Order in 1247, tradition held that Aylesford Priory was once the home of an early Prior General, Saint Simon Stock. The Carmelites at Aylesford began hoping that perhaps some of the relics of this holy saint might be brought back to his home community.

After the initial euphoria of the return, Malachy was faced with an immense task. Despite the good stewardship of the Hewitts, the buildings at The Friars were not in the best of conditions. The Great Courtyard was a mixture of cottage stores and stables, whilst the Pilgrims' Hall needed to be made good.

Parts of The Friars, such as the Cloisters, were in dire need of restoration when the Carmelites returned in 1949.

The Friars had been a private home for more than 400 years.

The Friars, Aylesford, in the early 1950s.

Besides the necessary repairs to the fabric, there was the need to define the apostolate of the priory. The Carmelites had come back to Aylesford after a break of 400 years, but what was to be their ministry in the Twentieth Century? Local clergy thought The Friars could be a secondary school, while the Prior General saw Aylesford as a centre for spirituality and the formation of student friars. What would be the main apostolate was to come – as Malachy would say – by "*indirections*".

In 1950 a group of pilgrims arrived at Aylesford from Ealing Abbey in London. They were caught by romance, mystery and beauty of the place, and word began to spread. Soon large groups of pilgrims were coming to The Friars every Sunday, and so by popular choice, rather than design of the Carmelites, Aylesford quickly developed into a centre for pilgrimage.

Cyril Cowderoy, Bishop of Southwark, on his first visit to Aylesford in 1950.

40

Visitors aside, the immediate task facing Malachy was to make the place liveable for a Carmelite community. Early memories of The Friars as a restored community are of penetrating damp and the need for kitchen facilities. On top of these problems there were building restrictions which made progress slow. The members of the Institute of Our Lady, who set up home in the Gatehouse, remembered the cold and the damp not helped by the proximity of the River Medway. Malachy had the support of his brother Elias, and Brother Anthony McGreal (also in Faversham), in raising the funds to begin the work of restoration. Fundraising was to be a constant reality for the rest of Malachy's life.

The Friars seen from the River Medway.

In the middle of settling into The Friars, Malachy had the responsibility of organising a pilgrimage to Rome for the Holy Year of 1950. The travel agency tasked with coordinating the trip proved totally incompetent, and at the last minute a new firm had to be found to cater for nearly 2,000 pilgrims. The Havas Agency stepped in and began to cope until the director of the firm took ill. However, with the help of volunteers, the pilgrims were looked after and reached Rome. When they got to the Eternal City there was a mix up with hotels, yet in the end most of the pilgrims enjoyed the experience; they were good-tempered and kept their sense of humour. Some of the pilgrims went by coach and were able to visit Lisieux and Chartres en route. Travelling was more of an adventure before the days of budget airlines and high-speed rail!

41

The Holy Year Pilgrimage of 1950 from Aylesford to Rome was led by Malachy's brother Kilian, the Carmelite Prior General, shown here being received in audience by Pope Pius XII.

Besides the energy needed to bring the pilgrimage to a successful conclusion, Malachy threw himself into the work taking place to restore the Pilgrims' Hall and the Great Courtyard. It was only as the buildings were examined that the extent of the restoration work began to be realised. Malachy felt he had stumbled into the project, not initially realising the enormity of the task. In the first year £25,000 was spent on *"acres of floors and roofs to be renewed"*; included in that sum was £5,000 for oak timbers. The workers had to be fed and sheltered, as had the members of the Institute and the friar community; all this with *"a footling kitchen and a cook of genius"*.

The dilapidated clocktower and watergate corner of the Great Courtyard, prior to the return of the Carmelites.

Malachy supervising restoration of the Great Courtyard.

42

Malachy decided to erect small statues over the doors in the Great Courtyard calling on the sculptural skills of Philip Lindsey Clark and his son Michael Clark. Malachy appealed for donations to cover the cost of the statues which came to £25 each.

The Great Courtyard at Aylesford, with examples of the doorway sculptures: St. Albert of Jerusalem and St. Mary Magdalene de'Pazzi, carved by Michael Clark.

Stumbling into buying a castle

Stumbling was one of Malachy's favourite words to describe unexpected developments and decisions. In his *Pilgrims' Newsletter* of March 1951 he wrote, *"we have stumbled again this time into buying Allington Castle for the Institute of Our Lady of Mount Carmel"*. It was a very big stumble, but answered a need as the Gatehouse at

43

Aylesford was not adequate for the Institute. Allington Castle, just two miles from The Friars, was a beautiful property dating from 1279.

Allington Castle, Kent.

The famous poet and diplomat, Sir. Thomas Wyatt, was born at Allington Castle in 1503. This portrait, created c.1535-37, is by Hans Holbein the Younger. Royal Collection, Windsor Castle.

It was a historical irony that Allington Castle should come under Carmelite ownership given that, at the Dissolution of the Monasteries, Henry VIII had granted Aylesford Priory to the Wyatts of Allington.

The Castle had been restored in the early part of the 20th Century by Lord Conway. Lord Conway's son-in-law, Mr. George Horsfield, now a widower, wanted to sell and move to warmer climes. He also hoped that the Castle might become a house of prayer. Malachy was due to lead a pilgrimage to Rome at Christmas 1950, and that enabled him to speak to the Prior General and get his approval. Father Kilian agreed that the Castle was most suitable; the only problem was how to pay for it. Despite other interested parties, Mr. Horsfield agreed to sell the Castle to the Carmelites for £15,000, accepting that payment would be in easy stages over a year from the time of taking possession. The purchase price included a gatehouse, four cottages, and some forty acres of land; as Malachy said, *"Our Lady has a good eye for a bargain"*.

44

Malachy, in his dealings with practicalities, saw Saint Teresa of Avila as an inspiration and Saint Joseph as the one who provides. He once told a bank manager that Saint Joseph was his surety; the manager was left speechless. In fact, Malachy was able to win the bank manager over, and seeing The Friars and Allington he was impressed.

Allington Castle was formally handed over to the Carmelites on Easter Sunday, 25th March 1951. Malachy arrived with a procession of friars and sisters to the great entrance door which was locked and barred. The Carmelites rang the ship's bell, and a question was heard from the other side of the side: '*What do you want?*'. Malachy answered dramatically, '*In the name of the Holy Trinity, we ask for possession of the Castle for Our Lady of Mount Carmel.*' The gates were unbolted, permission to enter was given, and the keys were formerly presented to the Order by the butler in Mr. Horsfield's presence. The keys were then laid on an altar and Mass was celebrated.

The sisters of the Institute of Our Lady of Mount Carmel soon settled in and began to make Allington Castle "*as clean as a new pin*", as Malachy wrote. Soon the Castle would hum with activity as it would house dignitaries attending the return to Kent of the relics of Saint Simon Stock.

In the meantime, Malachy was fundraising and travelling. One way of fundraising was donate a stone for The Friars. Stone cards were sent out, and donors could return the card with what would be the cost of a stone. At Whitsun Malachy led a pilgrimage to Lourdes and Lisieux to pray for help in all that was happening. The pilgrimage gave Malachy the chance to pray and be peaceful, and helped dispel the anxiety he had felt. On his return to Aylesford he found the stone cards had brought generous donations.

Return of the relics

No sooner was Malachy back from pilgrimage than he was off to France again, this time to Bordeaux to join celebrations for the feast of Saint Simon Stock.

45

Simon Stock was an Englishman who lived in the Thirteenth Century. He was one of the early Priors General of the Carmelite Order at a time when the hermits from Mount Carmel were adapting to life as mendicant friars. He was said to have been born in Kent, and to have lived at Aylesford. Little is known of Simon's life, but historians tell us that he died in Bordeaux (where he probably had family) and was buried there with a great reputation for holiness. Over the centuries

Saint Simon Stock's 'Scapular Vision' depicted in ceramic by Adam Kossowski at Aylesford Priory.

46

different medieval catalogues of saints and of priors general became conflated, and various legends about Simon Stock developed. The most famous was that he received a vision of the Blessed Virgin Mary, reputedly in 1251. According to this pious tradition, Our Lady blessed Simon's scapular, that is, the apron which goes over the head and shoulders, covering the front of the Carmelite habit. Mary's blessing reputedly came with a promise that those who wore the brown scapular of the Carmelites would receive her particular maternal protection, especially at the hour of death.

Wearing the brown scapular became hugely popular in Catholic cultures from the Seventeenth Century onwards, with many thousands of lay people wearing a miniature form of the habit round their neck as a devotional object. Historically-speaking we now know that the 'Scapular Vision' story is a complex mixture of legends and pious traditions, but at its heart is the very important truth that Mary, Our Lady, loves and cares for all people, and that everyone can benefit from some kind of connection to the Carmelite Family and its spirituality. Malachy was a great promoter of the Scapular devotion, encouraging people to offer a simple prayer to Mary as they put the cloth over their heads: "*Use me today.*"

Malachy travelled to Bordeaux in 1951 because, according to the popular reckoning, it was a milestone year: the 700th anniversary of the Scapular Vision. As Carmelite Prior of Aylesford, Simon Stock's former community, Malachy was a special guest, and he enjoyed splendid liturgies, eloquent sermons, and two banquets!

To the delight of the Carmelites, the Archbishop of Bordeaux had agreed to their request that some of the relics of Saint Simon Stock be 'translated' to his home community at Aylesford. Some of his mortal remains had already been sent to Carmelite and Discalced Carmelite communities in various parts of the world, but Aylesford was to be granted the special honour of housing a part of the saint's skull.

Much as Malachy enjoyed the celebrations in Bordeaux, he was a little anxious about how the celebrations would take place at Aylesford to mark the arrival of Saint Simon Stock's relics. There would be many

47

Saint Andrew's Cathedral in Bordeaux is where most of the mortal remains of Saint Simon Stock are venerated.

dignitaries and pilgrims to welcome, and it would all happen under the open sky; it would not be possible to fit everybody into the community house at The Friars.

Éamon de Valera, photographed in the 1930s.

Malachy's prayers for a successful event were answered; after torrential rain the weather was fine on the weekend of the arrival of the relics.

Among the dignities attending the celebrations were numerous bishops and heads of religious orders, as well as the Irish statesman Éamon de Valera who was Taoiseach (Prime Minister) and later President of Ireland, and who had a great devotion to the Carmelite brown scapular.

48

*Éamon de Valera at Aylesford with a Carmelite friar
and (right) Fr. Malachy.*

The celebrations began on Saturday 14th July with Mass celebrated by the Prior General in the solemn Carmelite Rite.

*The celebration of Mass in the Carmelite Rite during the
1951 translation of the Simon Stock relic.*

Then on the Sunday, Bishop Cowderoy of Southwark Diocese celebrated Mass with other bishops present, including Cardinal Adeodato Giovanni Piazza who was himself an Italian Discalced Carmelite friar and the Cardinal Protector of the Order. There was a slight hitch as the cardinal's robes had been mislaid at Heathrow Airport, but they arrived just at the crucial moment.

49

Cardinal Piazza at The Friars.

Most Reverend Paul-Marie-André Richaud, Archbishop of Bordeaux-Bazas, arriving in Aylesford with the relic of Saint Simon Stock. He was made a cardinal in 1958, and died a decade later. Éamon de Valera can be seen behind the archbishop.

50

The actual arrival of the relics took place in the afternoon. A huge crowd had gathered in Aylesford village for the event. In a kind ecumenical gesture, the Anglican Vicar of Aylesford made facilities available for vesting, and locals and visitors from far and wide joined together in the celebration.

The relics of Saint Simon Stock were carried across the old bridge in Aylesford village. Halfway over the bridge the Archbishop of Bordeaux handed the relics to Bishop Cowderoy, who processed with them to an altar at The Friars.

The procession of the relic of Saint Simon Stock over Aylesford bridge.

The handing over of the relics.

51

The procession of the relic of Saint Simon Stock through Aylesford village to The Friars.

52

The event attracted a massive gathering of pilgrims.

Once the reliquary had arrived at The Friars the pilgrims stood to hear a message from Pope Pius XII read out, and then an inspirational address by the bishop.

On the Monday, the Feast of Our Lady of Mount Carmel, Mass was celebrated by the cardinal

Cardinal Piazza presiding at the Eucharist in Aylesford. To his right is the Prior General Fr. Kilian Lynch. To his left is Fr. Bartolomé Xiberta, a Catalonian Carmelite renowned for his spirituality and devotion to Our Lady. He served as Assistant General of the Order, and became an important figure during the Second Vatican Council. The cause for his beatification is being considered.

53

The Pilgrims' Hall at Aylesford, following restoration.

The whole celebrations were witnessed by some 25,000 people, a logistical achievement with so many to be fed and accommodated. Allington Castle proved an ideal place to house distinguished visitors, while the Pilgrims' Hall at The Friars came into its own as a place of hospitality. Providing food and drink was no easy task as kitchen facilities were still quite meagre. The celebrations ended with a torchlight procession, while the relics found a temporary home in the small chapel in the cloisters. Malachy was blessed with so many volunteer helpers, and especially the sisters of the Institute.

In 1951 a temporary altar was established in the grounds of The Friars.

54

Illness and worries

With all the euphoria of the celebrations over, Malachy had to face financial realities. Among the commitments the Order had undertaken was paying for Allington Castle: £5,000 had been raised as a loan, but another £10,000 was needed by March 1952. The outlook seemed bleak, but Malachy held on to hope and his belief in divine providence.

However, financial worry and a heavy workload brought Malachy to hospital. His diabetes needed balancing, and despite his seeming strength his health was indifferent. He was happy to go along with the hospital regime, and he appreciated nursing care. One thing he did do was to heed a friend's advice and give up smoking, a decision that helped his health improve.

Meanwhile, Malachy could rely on more help from the international Carmelite Order, as the community of friars grew with brothers coming from Spain and Germany. Brothers Nuno and Simon were to prove invaluable helpers for the years to come, while Brother John Berridge was to give half-a-century of devoted service to Aylesford.

Writing in the summer of 1952, it is clear that worry about paying for Allington Castle was high on Malachy's agenda. Both the bank and solicitors were negative in their responses, and would have foreclosed if Allington's former owner, Mr. Horsfield, had not been understanding. Disaster was avoided with great help coming in the form of a £5,000 loan, and a visit to Dublin yielded £1,000 in donations.

Creative moments

Amid financial worries there were creative happenings at Aylesford. Through The Society of Catholic Artists, Malachy made contact with Adam Kossowski, a Polish artist. Adam had been a professor in the art department of Warsaw University. During the Second World War he fled east to escape Nazi occupation but ended up in Siberia at a Soviet labour camp. Fortunately, he was able to escape to England in 1943 where he settled as a refugee in London.

55

Adam's first commission was to be seven tempera paintings depicting episodes in the history of the Carmelite Order. These hang in the Prior's Hall by the Great Courtyard at The Friars.

The first panel painted by Adam Kossowski in the Prior's Hall at Aylesford depicts the origins of the Order, with hermits from Mount Carmel seeking approval for their way of life from Saint Albert, Latin Patriarch of Jerusalem in the early Thirteenth Century.

The panels narrate how the Carmelites came to Aylesford. This image depicts their arrival in England with the crusader knight Sir Richard de Grey, who gave them a small piece of land at his manor of Aylesford.

56

*Kossowski's panels depict the growth of Aylesford Carmelite Priory,
its Dissolution, and its Restoration.*

Adam was then asked to work in a medium that was new to him:
ceramics. He was commissioned to create fifteen miniature shrine-
scenes depicting the Mysteries of the Rosary. Malachy wrote of the
ceramics: *"They are an exciting revival of the 15th-Century medium
after the style of Della Robbias. They are lovely in their colour – they
have a primitive quality like his painting"*. The cost of the Rosary Way
was only £1,500.

Ceramics by Adam Kossowski on the Rosary Way at Aylesford Priory.

57

By now pilgrimages were more and more the apostolate of Aylesford with huge groups of children enlivening the place. Already Polish pilgrims were making their way to celebrate their faith.

Malachy preaching to pilgrims at The Friars.

Some 70 years after the Carmelites returned to Aylesford, pilgrims continue to pray along the Rosary Way.

When not busy welcoming pilgrims to Aylesford, Malachy continued to make his own pilgrimages elsewhere, Lourdes being a particularly favourite shrine.

*Malachy (front row) in Lourdes in 1952 with a Carmelite Pilgrimage (left)
and a group of Discalced Carmelite friars (right).*

Floods

1953 saw catastrophic flooding in the southeast of England. Aylesford,
being on the River Medway, experienced the force of a tidal surge.
It seems that the Priory had no radio, so everyone went to bed on
the fatal night unaware of the danger. Malachy was awakened at 2
a.m. by shouting, which at first he thought was Brother John having
a nightmare, but the reality of the situation soon became evident with
water everywhere. The Great Courtyard was awash, and a group of
retreatants found themselves trying to quell the flood. The farm area
was waist deep in water; the community got the pigs to dry ground,
while Brother Nono nearly lost his life trying to save the poultry.
Piles of timber meant for restoration work were washed away like
matchsticks, but in the end the damage was not as great as first
feared. Despite the floods, the restoration continued, though finance
was as ever a worry. Malachy's brother Kilian, the Prior General said,
"Ask me for anything except money!", and even his other brother,
Elias, had to call a halt to financial backing.

As the above account of the flood indicates, under Malachy's guidance
there was a thrust towards Aylesford Priory being self-sufficient with
livestock and poultry. Also, areas of the grounds were given over to

59

The impact of the 1953 floods in part of Essex.

growing vegetables, and a fair amount of land was pasture. A bakery was set up, with Brother Francis specialising in nutritious brown bread. What was also needed was an adequate kitchen able to feed friars, helpers, and pilgrims. These were just some of the day-to-day matters that needed direction and finance.

In the autumn of 1953, Malachy had an unexpected break. American friends wanted to visit Rome and see Fr. Kilian, the Prior General. The trip to Rome was by car, crossing the Alps to Florence and Siena. While in Rome, Malachy met Pope Pius who was most encouraging of Aylesford. Malachy was captivated by the Pope's personality and serenity.

On Malachy's return to Aylesford everything seemed lighter, with the kitchen complete and the bakery in full flow. Generous donations enabled work to be done at Allington Castle and Aylesford Gatehouse. There was, however, £7,000 still owing on Allington, and already plans were afoot to rebuild the chapel at Aylesford.

The vision of a chapel

Writing in the summer of 1954, Malachy was delighted at the great crowds of children who came to Aylesford for their special Mass on the Feast of Saint Simon Stock. Bishop Cowderoy celebrated on a cold, dry, day with an east wind. The logistics of the day included coping with 220 coaches.

60

1954 was a cold, wet, summer and the celebrations for 16th July – the Solemnity of Our Lady of Mount Carmel – looked as if they would be a washout. Seven thousand pilgrims had come for the feast, and ordinations to the priesthood. Despite a gloomy forecast, when the time came for Mass the sun appeared. However, a month later on the Solemnity of the Assumption, thunder and lightning were the accompaniment to the choir's singing as they processed to the altar. The storm clouds passed by, the rain fell elsewhere, and the pilgrims were able to pray without too much discomfort.

The unreliable weather made Malachy realise that a chapel had to be built on the site of where the chapel had been in the medieval priory. He wrote, *"A noble church will arise and the main altar will be set under a tower over topping the tallest trees."* He spoke of bells ringing-out to welcome pilgrims, and the great chapel being a shrine to Our Lady, honouring her Assumption, with a shrine to Saint Simon Stock in the crypt. Malachy had every confidence that a great church could be built, and he saw this as the real task of restoration at The Friars. The cost was not meant to be daunting, and the whole project could be finished in two years. Malachy was also determined that the chapel would be built in Kentish ragstone, the excellent quality local hard grey limestone, peculiarly suited to medieval-style architecture. The search for ragstone would not be easy, and yet by

On 8th September 1954 Bishop Cowderoy blessed the foundation stone marking the beginning of the restoration of a chapel at Aylesford dedicated to the Assumption of the Glorious Virgin Mary.

61

chance 500 tons of it was salvaged from an old mansion that was being demolished, along with fifty thousand peg-tiles. In a burst of optimism about the project and its completion, Malachy said it will *"jump up"*.

While all this vision of the new chapel was giving hope to all concerned, other buildings were jumping up at The Friars. The workshops were nearly complete; they included a laundry, pottery, carpenter's shop, weaving, printing, and stores. Malachy saw the workshops in a monastic light, blending work and prayer at Aylesford to the glory of God. Malachy was to encourage a number of workmen to become Carmelite friars, praising God by their skills. Many of those men were to stay in the Order, enabling Malachy's vision to be realised. Others would leave, but remained friends of the community. The Spanish brothers, Nono and Simon, saw to the cultivation of vegetables and the care of the grounds; they were tireless workers.

Brothers Benedict Reney and Michael McMullen at work at The Friars.

62

Brother Michael McMullen with Fr. Malachy Lynch on site during the construction of the chapel at The Friars.

A Catholic Scouts celebration at The Friars in 1954. The site had become an important centre for scouting in the 1920s, once visited by the founder of the Scout movement, Lord Baden-Powell.

63

Travels

Besides his hopeful vision for the future Malachy was busy travelling in the autumn of 1954, speaking at a conference in Spain, visiting Avila, and also Lisieux. He spent some time again in Lourdes and wrote of it *"Lourdes is the living Gospel, the pool of healing – down by the Grotto the guttering candles and that strange hush."* In a previous visit he found he was able to come off insulin and not have to be over-careful with his diet.

From Lourdes Malachy travelled to Spain and found medieval landscapes in Castile. Farming was still as it was in the Middle Ages, with donkeys and oxen. Malachy felt a great simplicity and intimacy

with the earth. While inspired by the great Carmelite Saint Teresa of Avila, the purpose of his visit was a Congress dedicated to Our Lady. Malachy was impressed by the commitment of the young people he met, and also the witness of those killed in the Spanish Civil War of the 1930s. General Franco was at the Congress, and Malachy – in common with many Catholics at that time – saw the General as the one who have saved Europe from Communism. History has shown how the Civil War produced acts of heroism and acts of cruelty on both sides. As victor, Franco proved himself unforgiving of the opposition, and the wounds of that period are still to be healed. However, Malachy saw Franco as the bulwark against the radical Left, and he was devoted to Our Lady of Mount Carmel.

Some of the personal effects of Carmelites who were martyred for their faith during the Spanish Civil War, on display in the Discalced Carmelite Friary in Toledo. The killing of dozens of members of the Carmelite Family in Spain, within Malachy's own lifetime, made a deep impression on him.

64

Worn out and ill

At the beginning of 1955 Malachy collapsed and seemed near death. He was so ill that his brother Elias came over from Faversham in the middle of the night to anoint him. He was to spend six weeks at l'Esperance Hospital in Eastbourne where he was nursed back to health. Malachy was grateful to have such good care.

The Esperance Hospital in Eastbourne.

When Malachy returned to Aylesford he found himself overwhelmed by financial problems arising from the restoration work. The overdraft was £25,000. Desperate measures were the order of the day, and yet he felt utterly exhausted with all these pressures coming on top of his illness. Elias was worried at Malachy's state of mind. He wrote to fellow Carmelite, Pat Geary, on 6th April: "*We have to be careful about Malachy, ideas tumble through his head at such a rate that one is in danger of knocking the other out.*"

Also writing to Pat Geary, Malachy confessed that his nerves were in a shocking state because he was still feeling ill and was worried, facing into so much responsibility. The most radical idea was to sell Allington Castle to Lord Bossom, then a local Member of Parliament; the asking price was £40,000. The newly-built workshop block at Aylesford could become a school. Malachy also had ideas about the historic barns at the entrance to The Friars. However, Lord Bossom would only offer £11,000, and the proposal about a school was soon seen as a non-starter. In all the talk of selling the Castle, the Sisters of the Institute who lived there were not part of the conversation. Malachy did have the help of Harry Freed, a land agent who acted *pro bono*, and Philip Ardizzone, a solicitor who again was generous with advice.

Writing just after leaving hospital, Malachy remarked: *"The aftermath of an illness is worse than an illness itself – there are times when black blots black out, so dark and depressing seems the outlook – all this has to do with the body, and then the light comes again."*

Not all was gloom; the workshops at Aylesford were finished, and Fr. Brocard Sewell set up his printing press. Publishing as The Carmelite Press and Saint Albert's Press, Brocard was

to produce fine editions using a hand press, cultivating relationships with various writers and artists. Brother Aloysus, a German carpenter, was training postulants (would-be friars), and David Leach had started the pottery, beginning a tradition that still holds good today. David produced some wonderful glazes which would be passed on by Brother Michael. Malachy saw the activities in the workshops as continuing the spiritual rhythm of work and prayer. He also regarded the artwork of Aylesford Priory as enhancing the spiritual nature of the site, famously describing The Friars as *"a prayer in stone."*

Fr. Brocard Sewell, painted by Jane Percival.

As regards building the new chapel at The Friars, the Carmelite Prior General, Fr. Kilian, counselled his brother that no construction should begin until a third of the cost was in hand. Malachy realised that he would have to be patient, and there was a need to scale-down his ambitious plans. He realised that the church would have to be most simple, and not beyond the skill of his own masons. He saw the building-work as an act of dedication on the part of the craftsmen.

66

Aylesford Pottery stoneware tea set designed by David Leach, O.B.E., covered in a tenmoku glaze.

About this time Malachy reflected on the outreach of the *Pilgrims' Newsletter*, which now had a circulation of 20,000 and had reached its twenty-first number. The first newsletter had been sent to the 1,500 pilgrims who had gone to Rome with the Carmelites for the Holy Year of 1950.

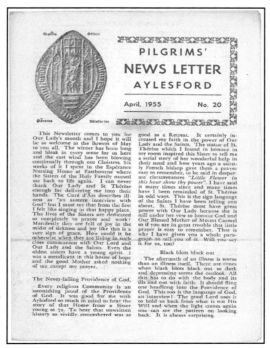

The Pilgrims' Newsletter from April 1955.

67

As we have remarked, that pilgrimage was dogged by problems, but the pilgrims asked to keep contact and be a support to the Order. In the five years since Rome, so much had been achieved – the Great Courtyard was fully restored.

The Great Courtyard at The Friars, Aylesford, as it appears today.

During 1955 Malachy came to the end of his six years (two terms) as Prior of the Carmelite friar community. In fact, he had been Prior in Wales for twelve years before coming to Aylesford. The new Prior at The Friars was Patrick Russell, who had been a student with Malachy in Rome and then ministered in America. Pat, as he was called, was a gentle and sensitive person, and recognised that Malachy's ministry should not be hindered. Pat focussed his attention on the life of the Carmelite community, which included novices. He gave special care to the liturgy, and he was remembered by Brocard Sewell as *"Good Prior Russell."*

Malachy used time to visit Hulne in Northumberland, which – like Aylesford – was founded as a desert house by hermits from Mount Carmel in 1242. The ruins of Hulne Priory, on the estate of the Duke of Northumberland at Alnwick Castle, are quite impressive. Malachy saw Hulne as a place for contemplative prayer, and dreamed that one day it would be restored as a place of worship and bring values of prayer to the community.

Malachy found the England of his day spiritually desolate, and he saw the old parish churches and cathedrals as mere monuments for tourists to gape and gaze at. Perhaps he would be pleased to see how those same cathedrals have done much since his time to restore dignified worship in the Anglican Church.

68

The ruins of Hulne Priory in Northumberland, the first foundation of the Carmelite Order in England.

Irish interlude

In the spring of 1956 Malachy paid a visit to Ireland, the first for some years. The occasion was the visit of his sister, who was the Superior of the Mercy Nuns in Australia. They had not seen each other for some forty years. Malachy was only fourteen when his sister left home, and in his memory she was "a *tall girl, good looking, a bit easy mannered, and depths of something in her.*" When they were reunited, he wrote, "*I found myself looking down upon a small woman not much of her in it but all there and very forthcoming … it took me a long time to unearth Ciss.*" They were able to visit Wicklow and the small church at Askanagap where the family had worshipped. Malachy was able to celebrate Mass for the neighbours, and rejoice in listening to the rich speech of the mountain men. He then travelled to the Boyne Valley to find other relatives. The journey was not without incident, as Deidre his niece, driving out of Dublin, avoided a collision "*in a most sudden way.*

Malachy had a colourful use of language, and he was always fascinated by people. He had an all-absorbing way of seeing people. Women, especially nuns, impressed him. Speaking of some Polish

69

A section of the Boyne Valley, Ireland.

sisters who came to Aylesford in the summer of 1956, he observed: *"They were aristocratic in the most high spiritual sense – They all seemed to possess a noble dignity. I have never seen habits and faces and bearing more beautiful, like faces in the canvasses of the old masters – the grace of God shining through the flesh."*

1956 was a year when the savagery of the Soviet reaction to the Hungarian uprising shocked people in the West. Malachy felt great sadness for the suffering people, and saw hope in their courage.

A tank rolls through Budapest during the Hungarian Revolution of 1956. Such current events greatly distressed Malachy.

70

Neglect of God and indifference were at the heart of these horrors. In the middle of the tyranny the Poles were still able to honour God and Mary, but in Budapest alone 20,000 met their death.

The visit to Ireland gave Malachy hope; the people seemed to have a great sense of life, and the children impressed him with their spontaneous spirituality, with a child he met lighting a candle for the world.

Mother Mary Martin.

Whilst in Ireland he was able to visit Drogheda where a most modern hospital was being built by the Medical Missionaries of Mary. This was an order of religious sisters who were all doctors, nurses, and midwives, bringing their medical gifts to the missions. Drogheda was the mother house, and home of the founder Mother Mary Martin. Malachy marvelled at this centre of excellence, and at the calm and gentleness of Mother Mary. When Malachy asked her if she worried about money, her answer was that if she did *"I should regard myself as greatly wanting in faith."*

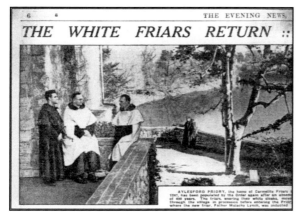

A news-cutting from the time of the Carmelites' return to Aylesford shows Whitefriars in the River View Garden. The friar in the middle is Bede Caine.

It was a salutary lesson in trusting divine providence which needed to be taken to heart. In fact, the overdraft facing Aylesford was down from £9,000 to £3,000, and if anyone was worrying it was Bede Caine, the community bursar, who was also an excellent musician with a great gift for plainchant. Moreover, the pottery was flourishing and the

71

printing press was busy. Work was also going on to turn the space over the workshops into guestrooms for pilgrims.

Healing care

Over the years many pilgrims came to Aylesford seeing a cure for their illnesses, and Malachy gave time and care especially to families whose children were sick. A number of children with Leukaemia found great support at Aylesford, and Malachy gave them time, believing that prayer could give the strength needed to overcome the illness. Indeed, about this time a little boy called Peter responded to treatment and regained his health. Malachy visited a patient in a mental health unit; he was shocked by the size of the place and how crowded the wards were. Despite the efforts of the management the patients seemed lost and desolate. Most of the patients were elderly and seemed to need love and care. In Malachy's mind they seemed abandoned by families, asking the State to do more than it could ever manage. What was needed was the experience of loving pity.

The Carmelite students and novices at Aylesford in 1957.

Fátima

In the spring of 1957 Malachy went on pilgrimage to Fátima in Portugal. It was the 40th anniversary of the apparitions of Our Lady to three peasant children. Malachy arrived at the shrine after midnight when everything was somewhat chaotic, but with the help of a Dominican friar, Malachy reached Casa Beato Nuno, the newly-opened Carmelite hostel. It was 12th May, the vigil of the anniversary of the apparitions, and thousands of pilgrims were settling down to sleep among the rocks and boulders around the sanctuary area. Malachy found his time in Fátima quite amazing. He later had memories of solemn celebrations, of Mass, and an abundance of bishops in mitres and copes. The whole experience was almost too much to absorb. What was more impressive was the stream of pilgrims walking in bare feet and carrying bundles on their heads.

The shrine of Our Lady of Fátima where the Blessed Virgin Mary appeared (on one occasion dressed as Our Lady of Mount Carmel) to three peasant children in 1917.

Malachy went on to the Portuguese town of Coimbra where one of the Fátima visionaries, Lúcia Santos, had become a Discalced Carmelite nun a decade earlier. As Malachy journeyed he marvelled at the natural beauty around him transformed by the brightness of the sun. Coimbra is famous for its university, but Malachy's reason for going there was a hope to meet Sister Lúcia. The Prioress explained that

73

Lúcia did not receive visitors, but assured Malachy that the visionary would pray for the apostolate of Aylesford.

Lúcia Santos as a child, and as a Carmelite nun.

Malachy returned from his pilgrimage refreshed, and delighted to find the overdraft down to £1,000. It seemed to him possible that a start could be made in building the chapel in the autumn, and it would be finished by 1960.

In the summer of 1957 an international Scout jamboree was held at Buckmore Park just up the road from The Friars. Over a period of three days the scouts came to celebrate Mass, with a number of bishops from Britain and France present. The weather was unkind, with mud the order of the day. On the Saturday of the jamboree there was a formal lunch in the Pilgrims Hall with the Duke of Norfolk, the Chief Scout Lord Rowallen, and the Archbishop of Westminster among the guests. Malachy fell into conversation with a French bishop who pronounced the Carmelites to be *"Absolument-unique!"*

Iberian interlude

Malachy's health was still fragile, with the pressure of work tiring him out, since he gave of himself generously to the pilgrims. He was told, for the sake of his health, to go back to Portugal and stay for a month. He was also asked to keep an eye out for stonemasons and potters who might come back to Aylesford with him and work on the restoration of The Friars.

Malachy went by train through France, but when he got to Irun he found he needed a visa to enter Spain. More by luck than anything

74

SEGRETERIA DI STATO
DI SUA SANTITA

N.401.523

Dal Vaticano, li **May 23, 1957**

Very Reverend and dear Father Prior,

When the hallowed remains of St. Simon Stock were being solemnly carried back to the home of his earthly sojourn, the Holy Father signified His paternal interest in the event by addressing a Pontifical Letter to the Prior General of the Order of Carmelites, and ever since then He has closely followed the progress of the re-established Monastery at Aylesford.

It has indeed been a source of deep satisfaction for His Holiness to note the success which has attended the zealous efforts of yourself and your confreres. Not only has the material reconstruction of the historic Monastery been almost completed, but Aylesford has once again become an important source of spiritual life and a precious centre of apostolic activity, both amongst Catholics and amongst those outside the true fold.

In expressing His felicitations on this admirable record of achievement, the Pontiff renders heartfelt thanks to Almighty God for the bountiful blessings He has bestowed. He cherishes the prayerful hope that the Apostolate of Aylesford may continue to reap an ever more abundant harvest of spiritual fruits, and in particular that an increasing number of the faithful in Mary's Dowry may ensure for themselves the special help and protection of their heavenly Mother by devoutly wearing Her Scapular.

With that prayer, the Holy Father cordially imparts to you, to the members of your Community, and to all those who collaborate with you in promoting the Apostolate of Aylesford, His paternal Apostolic Benediction.

Gladly do I assure you of my high esteem and cordial regard, and I remain,

Yours sincerely in Christ,

[signature]
Substitute

Very Rev. Malachy Lynch, O.Carm.
Prior, The Friars

AYLESFORD, Kent.

A letter from the Vatican to Malachy in 1957.

else, he was able to get a visa from the Consul and catch a train by the skin of his teeth. Malachy travelled third class, enjoying the theatre of his fellow passengers, and almost twenty hours later he was in Fátima once again.

When Malachy reached Casa Beato Nuno, he found two friends waiting to welcome him: Dr. Alan Barnsley and his wife Edwina. The Barnsleys lived in Maidstone, very near to Aylesford, and had come to know The Friars and Malachy. Alan Barnsley was a successful novelist writing under the pseudonym of Gabriel Fielding. The little group enjoyed exploring the wooded countryside, and were fascinated by the villagers they met, living in great simplicity and great dignity. With his friends Malachy enjoyed an *al fresco* meal of sardines, bread and wine; it reminded him of the meal prepared by Jesus for his friends in John's Gospel. Malachy realised that it was in these woods that the three Fátima peasant children had had their visions, with the family house nearby unchanged from how it had been in 1917. Lúcia's sister still lived in the family home, middle-aged and stately, *"with quiet in her and a great wisdom."*

At the end of the holiday, during which Malachy had also spent time with relatives in Porto and Lisbon, he headed back to Paris by Pullman. He felt far from comfortable, complaining of *"a strange feeling not unlike death."* Malachy chose the second sitting for lunch, but the meal was running late. As he queued he prayed the rosary, and as it was Friday he had to ask for an omelette in place of meat. All the time he felt uncomfortable at the conspicuous consumption around him. He fell into conversation with an industrialist whom he found desperately negative. Malachy tried to get him to open up to some spiritual feeling, but all he could see were empty masques and depths of sadness in the midst of luxury. My interpretation of Malachy's account of the episode is that he felt so alienated because he was in a world that seemingly had no point of contact with his own values.

While Malachy was away from Aylesford, the architect Adrian Gilbert Scott was yet again revising plans for the chapel. Adrian Scott was an English ecclesiastical architect who came from a large family of

76

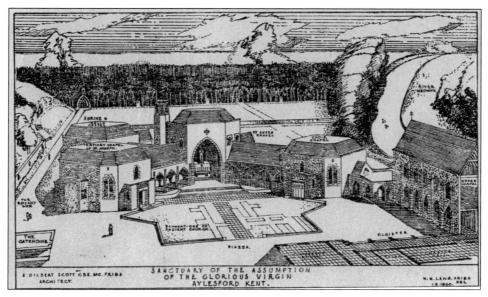

Adrian Gilbert Scott's drawing of the proposed shrine.

Initial stages of construction of the Main Shrine in 1958.

77

renowned draftsmen. Together Adrian and Malachy had conceived the idea of building a number of linked-chapels and a Main Shrine with a large open-air piazza in front that could (weather-permitting) accommodate large numbers of pilgrims in the summer pilgrimage season. Adrian Scott had been patient, having to keep on producing drawings only for new ideas from the Carmelites to demand a fresh approach. However, by the spring of 1958 agreement was reached and a way forward was possible. I remember chancing upon a heated conversation between Kilian and Malachy, with Kilian obviously frustrated at the delays and changes of plan. On this occasion there were no clerical niceties observed between William (Fr. Malachy) and Edward (Fr. Kilian) Lynch: it was two brothers being frank and heated. It was 'Bill' and 'Ned' thrashing it out!

A day in court

Later on in 1958 Malachy had his day in court. In December 1953 he had welcomed to Aylesford a couple of weavers who were members of the Carmelite Third Order, and they were enthusiastic to contribute to the life of The Friars. However, relationships floundered and they sued the Carmelite friars. The weavers wanted their day in court rather than settle. The case was heard beginning on 30th April and lasted three days. Malachy was both nervous yet fascinated by the legal proceedings, and found the judge's robes to be like those of a well-groomed bishop. Malachy, wearing a black suit rather than habit and white cloak, felt more like an undertaker. He was in a kind of pulpit and yet – strangely for him – could hardly say a word. Fortunately for the friars, Mrs. Wallace and Pauline Healy provided articulate and calm witnesses. The trial awoke in Malachy a deeper respect for Common Law, Magna Carta, and the great humanist and legal mind Saint Thomas More. Aylesford Priory was fortunate in having as its defence counsel Don Harvey, a graduate of Trinity College, Dublin. He had come to Catholicism through retreats at Aylesford, and also thanks to his friendship with the aforementioned Dr. Barnsley which dated back to university days. The trial came to an end with an exonerating judgement from the Court, much to everyone's relief, as it was widely seen as a vindictive action against the friars.

78

The north-east corner of the Great Courtyard at The Friars c.1958.

Change at Allington

At the same time as the trial, a significant change was happening at Allington Castle. The members of The Institute of Our Lady of Mount Carmel were leaving the Castle for a new foundation at Chislehurst. The Sisters, as they were known, had been generous in supporting so much of the restoration at Aylesford. In the early days nearby Allington had become their home, enabling the Institute to grow and also for the Castle to develop as a retreat house. However, the members of the Institute undertook a period of discernment which was to change their future. Secular Institutes such as theirs had been established in Church Law in 1947, only shortly before the Carmelites were to return to Aylesford. With the re-establishment of friars at Aylesford, it seemed natural for the Carmelite Family to develop a community of religious sisters to live and work alongside them. However, the charism of a Secular Institute is for its members to live the evangelical counsels of chastity, poverty and obedience whilst 'in the world', unlike members of a Religious Institute who live in a community. As a Secular Institute the Allington 'Sisters' felt that they were meant to be more 'in the world'; the lifestyle at the Castle was far too monastic for them to live their vocation properly. Also, relationships between Malachy and the Institute had become

79

strained, especially when negotiations to sell the Castle in 1955 had not included the Institute.

The Institute flourished after it left Allington. Now it is called The Leaven, calling to mind the Gospel image of yeast that enables bread to rise even though it is unseen. Today The Leaven is a significant part of the Carmelite Family in Britain, and the friars owe a debt of gratitude to the members of the Institute who were so generous in their commitment in those early days: Joan and Frieda Swingler, along with Norah Melia, Guida Pryor, and Teresa Grice.

Members of The Leaven (Institute of Our Lady of Mount Carmel) on retreat in 2011.

Collaborative ministry: This painting by Adam Kossowski depicts various branches of the Carmelite Family, including friars and Lay Carmelites, gathered together in honour of Mary and Jesus.

80

At this juncture the Prior General was all for selling Allington, but agreed to see it become a centre of apostolate for Carmelite Tertiaries, and an 'Open Door' welcoming those searching for faith. Malachy put energy into this new phase of the Castle's life, declaring *"I love it nearly as much as Aylesford."*

By this time Malachy was 59, and conscious that his time was limited. He perceived in the Carmelite Third Order a source of help to Church and Society that could not always be given by the friars.

Help was certainly needed at Aylesford so that the initial work on the chapel could begin. Laying foundations meant sinking piles into the ground to counteract the mud, as the building was so close to

Piles being sunk to stabilise the ground for the Main Shrine and chapels.

the River Medway. I remember, along with my fellow novices, pushing barrow-loads of cement to pour into the piles. Enough work was completed that on 20th July 1958, Solemnity of the Prophet Elijah, it was possible to lay the foundation stone that had been blessed four years earlier.

During the summer Malachy appealed again to the pilgrims for support. His slogans were biblical. He wrote *"The stones are crying out"*, recalling the words of Jesus to his disciples. Hope gave new significance to the words of Psalm 51 – *"Let me hear joy and gladness; let the bones that you have crushed rejoice"* – describing as *"Ossa humiliata"* the skeletons of medieval friars and benefactors buried beneath the feet of the pilgrims. Malachy would preach at least three times a day with his white cloak wrapped round him. He would be exhausted by the effort, and left weak by his diabetes.

Malachy preaching at Aylesford.

Lourdes and Aylesford

Later in the summer Malachy again visited Lourdes, finding inspiration and renewed energy. He was affected in October 1958 by the death of Pope Pius XII, whom he believed lived the primacy of love and brought humanity into what could become an institutional Church. Pius was a living-out of love and light in dark days, and for Malachy the Holy Father seemed to be a mystic and almost superhuman. Malachy's comment on Pius' successor, Pope John XXIII, was to see him as homely and kind – of good farming stock – almost making the Italian Pontiff an honorary Wicklow man!

Malachy had great admiration and affection
for Popes Pius XII and John XXIII.

Alongside all this reflection about the Church in Rome, Malachy could say that the church in Aylesford was *"jumping up!"* A team of fifteen workers were on the site – from England, Portugal and Italy – and all enthused by the project.

Workers constructing the Shrine area at The Friars.

82

Meanwhile, inspired by Lourdes, Malachy was dreaming that a 'City of Mary' would emerge at Allington with houses for large families. Just for good measure, he could announce the fact that the sewage pumps were working!

As the New Year emerged, Malachy was happy to see progress on the Main Shrine and chapels at Aylesford. From his room he could hear the sound of the mason's hammer. He saw the mason's craft as disciplined, patient, and with the quality of prayer; all done for the glory of God. On a more practical level the Managing Director of SGB Limited loaned enough scaffolding to keep the work going for a year, while Cubbitt's loaned a cement mixer, and Gleeson's also loaned equipment. Such generosity from supportive businesses saved a considerable sum of money.

The spring of 1959 saw Malachy back at L'Esperance Hospital in Eastbourne. Gastric flu played havoc with his diabetes, and he was critically ill. Rest and a chance to read helped him back to balance.

A feature of Malachy's writing is his love of colourful speech, especially if it were Wicklow folk speaking. Speech for him was courtesy, kindness, and many subtleties besides. It is sad when people lose their local accent to replace it with Standard English. While convalescing, Malachy was able to read the letters of Hilaire Belloc, edited by Robert Speaight. Belloc's opinions resonated well with Malachy, who respected the writer's forthrightness (a good comment by Malachy): the Catholic Church is not a museum or a perpetual debating society.

Writing in the spring of 1959, Malachy was happy to see that overdraft down by £4,000, and report that the now bank manager was sympathetic. Work on the Main Shrine was going well and help was still forthcoming from Catholic contractors Gleeson's, McAlpine's and Cubbit's, as well as SGB. Already Malachy was dreaming of the artwork that Adam Kossowski and Michael Clark would execute: *"The giant is beginning to walk but he still needs a mighty lot of help."*

Malachy was still far from well, and while he wanted to emulate Teresa of Avila (who did not worry much about her body), he was

83

far from having her wisdom. He struggled with diabetes, as it can obscure your outlook, fill you with alarms over nothing, and reduce you to eating lettuce! Despite his illness, Malachy could see progress on the building, huge crowds of pilgrims coming to Aylesford, and the generous support of Bishop Cowderoy who identified with the whole restoration project. All this helped lift Malachy's depression.

The construction of the Main Shrine at Aylesford Priory, c.1958.

A visit to Dachau

Later in the summer of 1959, Malachy was invited by philanthropist and Catholic convert Leonard Cheshire to spend an all-night vigil of prayer at Dachau concentration camp in Germany. In Malachy's mind Dachau evoked images from Dante's *Inferno*; it was a city of the dead, a strange lost world. He saw the cruelty that had been inflicted as satanic, not just in Dachau but also in Auschwitz and so many other camps.

The priests' barracks in Dachau lodged 2,579 Catholic clergy who were incarcerated here for their opposition to the Nazi regime of Adolf Hitler.

84

For Malachy there was a special reason for his going to Dachau, namely to honour the memory of fellow Carmelite friar Titus Brandsma, who died in the camp in 1942. Malachy had known Titus in Ireland in 1935, and from when he had visited Titus's town of Nijmegen on his way back from Rome in 1934. Malachy paints an evocative picture of Titus: the academic; the lover of Teresa; the mystic; the kind pastor; and someone who (in the Dutch style) loved his cigars (a way of offering incense to God!). For Malachy (and later the whole Church), Titus was a saint in the camp at Dachau. The nurse who killed Titus with a lethal injection was overcome by his holiness, and later testified to his holiness. For Malachy, Dachau was where the blood of martyrs truly is the seed of the Church. Titus also brought to mind Edith Stein – a philosopher, Discalced Carmelite nun, and martyr – who died in Auschwitz. Being born Jewish, Edith said she died for her people. Such a sentiment prompted a lovely quote from Johannes Neuhäusler, the auxiliary bishop of Munich who was in Dachau for four years: *"Only prayer and sacrifice dissolves hate."*

Titus Brandsma and Edith Stein: two Carmelite martyrs of the Second World War.

Generous support

Back in Aylesford the building work was progressing well with the tower over the Main Shrine almost complete. Malachy climbed the sixty steps to the top and was rewarded with a bird's-eye view of the golden autumn sun. Meanwhile work was going ahead in the farmyard, and the new block with extra accommodation for pilgrims was nearly completed. As noted earlier, Malachy was keen to be self-

85

sufficient with vegetables and milk, though with the numbers to be fed it could be a tall order.

By now Carmelite sisters from Spain were in charge of the kitchen, a role they were to fulfil wonderfully for some thirty years. I remember Sister Carmelo always with a smile, even at hectic moments. The Spanish sisters lived in the Gatehouse, which was extended to include a small chapel and a lovely courtyard.

The Carmelite Sisters of the Sacred Heart ('Spanish Sisters') outside their home at Aylesford, the Gatehouse.

The building work was held up at this stage as rods and mesh for the foundations were needed. Mr. Gleeson sent five tons of rods and the necessary steel mesh. Most of the work, apart from working the ragstone, was done by volunteers, including Clifford Jones the Managing Director of SGB. Malachy saw all this help as living out the true spirit of mendicant friars, that is, begging brothers who rely on the generous support of others.

The bills for all this work were mounting up, but when the crisis was at its bleakest, large donations eased the situation. The bank manager - unaware of the crisis when he saw a good bottom line – wrote to congratulate Malachy, who paradoxically felt he had somehow lost his *raison d'être*.

Malachy preaching to a group of pilgrims on the Rosary Way at Aylesford.

86

A new Prior

In the November 1959 *Pilgrims' Newsletter* Malachy made an important announcement: his brother Kilian, who had just finished his time as Prior General of the whole Carmelite Order, had elected to live in Aylesford and would be the new Prior of the house. Kilian asked Malachy to be in charge of pilgrimages, and give time to Allington and its apostolate.

So a new chapter in Malachy's life began. He was just 60, and had carried the responsibility of Aylesford for the best part of ten years. This new phase of his life was to be a creative time, as well as a time of illness, and at moments he found it not easy being no longer responsible for the whole endeavour.

Writing in January 1960, there is a wonderful contrast in Malachy's correspondence between anxieties over suppliers and lyrical comments about the Mass. Winter – with its cold, dark, stormy days – did little to lift the spirits. There was a crisis with heating and lighting, and the architect was not happy at delays. Fortunately, a firm that could help was in the area building a motorway, and they had the necessary equipment to finish the building. They did the work for nothing. The same happened with electrics; the firm had a Catholic boss who gave his services for free. Wingett's gave another cement mixer, and a lorry was donated. With all these resources on site, the architect had all he needed to continue the work. Then – as icing on the cake – a Hillman Station Wagon was donated as the Austin A40 van was on its last legs.

Malachy believed that what was most valuable – the best gift of all – was the way in which the volunteers joined in the prayer life of the Carmelite community, celebrating Mass together to start the day's work, and ending with prayer in the evening: "*It is the living Christ to whom they are joined in the Mass who gives them immense power – the Mass begins a day – there are no boundaries to the infinite reach of Christ.*"

Reflecting back on his days in Faversham, Malachy could see, with the help of time, how coming to that "*poor mission*" had enabled Aylesford to return to the Carmelites. It had seemed quite a fantasy in 1926, but Malachy realised that Fr. John Cogan had possessed great foresight and commitment in giving his trust over to God's providence.

By July 1959 enough progress had been made that it was possible to celebrate the ordination of Fr. Joseph Kelly in the partly-built Main Shrine.

Portugal again featured in Malachy's life, and he nurtured an ever-growing love for that country. He was willing to go as a chaplain on a weekend pilgrimage to Fátima over the period of the 13th May feast. The weekend was chaotic with terrible turbulence during the flight, and then rain, heavy traffic, and getting lost. Fortunately, Malachy found an *en suite* room in the Carmelite hospice Casa Beata Nuno where he could sleep and be recharged in order to lead the pilgrims in exuberant celebrations. Malachy was very conscious of how poor Portugal was at that time, under the paternalistic rule of a dictatorial Prime Minister, António de Oliveira Salazar. Malachy found himself taken by the gypsy women with their babies, begging and praying, and with a beauty that seemed so delicate.

Great progress

1960 saw great progress with the Shrine sanctuary at Aylesford. In August, on the Feast of the Assumption, Michael Clark's great statue of Our Lady arrived. With the help and direction of the foreman Percy Kitchen, a devoted worker at The Friars, it was fixed to its pedestal. The statue was 9 feet high with gold leaf lacquered judiciously. Meanwhile, the pottery was making blue tiles and flames for a ceramic background.

88

Michael Clark's statue of the Glorious Virgin of the Assumption.

Malachy was lyrical in his feelings about the building, about the commitment of the workers, and even about the very stones and timber. He also sang the praises of Michael Clark the sculptor whom he saw as a man of faith. Again, Malachy realised the privilege of working with Adam Kossowski, whose ceramics are the jewel of restored Aylesford. Adam's time in a Soviet Gulag had left him with severe rheumatism that threatened his ability to work, but by giving up milk he found freedom from pain and could glorify God with his ceramics.

In 1960 Dachau was again part of Malachy's travels; this time it was in the context of the 37th International Eucharistic Congress at Munich. As a result of the all-night prayer vigils at Dachau, a memorial chapel had been built there by the Catholic Church, dedicated to the Mortal Agony of Christ. This was also the time for acts of reparation, and

The Mortal Agony of Christ Memorial Chapel at Dachau.

89

great contingents of young people came to offer reparation. What also impressed Malachy was the way the people of Munich had given priority to rebuilding churches in the post-war reconstruction. A few years later, a monastery of Carmelite nuns would be built at Dachau.

In all his travels and activity Malachy was constantly finding new sources of inspiration and challenge. The writings of Henri Bergson, the French Philosopher who died in 1941, impressed Malachy, especially what he had to say about mystics, and that love was at the centre of creation, like a terrible fire at the heart of the universe. Bergson remained a Jew but hoped a Catholic priest could be at his funeral; the mystics were caught up in the love of God for all people. Bergson, with his openness, helped Malachy to recognise the power of God's work in this philosopher who had climbed the mount of God's love.

Henri Bergson.

Allington: an 'Open Door'

Now Malachy was no longer Prior of Aylesford, he spent more time at Allington Castle, and this led him to reminisce as to how he first came into contact with the place. He had initially seen Allington as sinister, having been the home of Sir Thomas Wyatt whom, in 1538 at the Dissolution of the Monasteries, had received Aylesford Priory for services rendered, from Thomas Cromwell, chief minister to King Henry VIII.

Malachy had walked over to the Castle from Aylesford and befriended Mr. Horsfield, who had inherited the Castle from Lord Conway. The sight of Malachy in his habit had excited Mr. Horsfield, and thus began a relationship that led to the Carmelites buying the Castle. With this transaction Mr. Horsfield had a sense that an injustice to the Carmelites had been put right, and he was delighted that Allington Castle should become a house of prayer. Malachy saw the Carmelites at the Castle as offering 'The Apostolate of the Open Door', welcoming people from all backgrounds, and making it a

90

place of retreat and prayer. Malachy was able to divert energies towards restoring and developing the Castle, looking for furniture, paintings and tapestries to cover the bare walls, especially in the Great Hall.

In the middle of floods Malachy went on a pilgrimage to Lisieux which was not without its moments. First of all, he forgot his passport, but ended a frustrating journey by trying to be philosophical about it. He was able to celebrate Mass in the Carmel at Lisieux, and to remind the nuns there of their promise of prayer for Aylesford.

The Great Hall in Allington Castle after it passed from Carmelite to private hands in 1999.

Lisieux Carmel where St. Thérèse lived as an enclosed Carmelite nun until her death in 1897.

The great Benedictine abbey of Bec is near Lisieux, and Malachy was impressed by its size. Bec was the home of Lanfranc and Anselm, great medieval Archbishops of Canterbury. Despite the bitter cold the visit made a good impression on Malachy, especially reflecting on the sublime writings of Anselm. The pilgrimage again closed in confusion with Malachy ending up in Paris instead of Le Havre. What struck him powerfully was the presence of so many rough sleepers in the Paris Metro. He was aware of the work among the homeless then being done by Abbé **Pierre,** and realised that spiritual poverty was more insidious than material lack.

Back at Allington, Bishop Cowderoy gave Malachy some time and in their chat expressed his support for Aylesford and Allington. While they were talking an urgent message came saying that they were needed at Aylesford. The bishop drove Malachy over to The Friars where an elderly lady wanted to help pay off the Carmelites' overdraft, to the tune of £7,000! She was conscious of the worry it must cause. On top of that there was a $4,000 cheque from the States

91

awaiting Malachy, who felt that Saint Joseph had been providing in his role as 'Principal Protector of the Carmelite Order'.

In the meantime, there was good news too from the artists Michael Clark and Adam Kossowski. For his statue of the Glorious Virgin, Michael had won a medal for the best work of sculpture from the Royal British Society of Sculptors. He was now making a model of his proposed statue of Saint Joseph. Adam would work with Michael on St. Joseph's Chapel at The Friars, and he was also drawing his angels for the Main Shrine. Adam was now free of arthritis and conscious of the great task he had been given.

Adam Kossowski supervising the laying of the sanctuary floor in St. Joseph's Chapel.

St. Joseph's Chapel at Aylesford Priory beautifully blends the artistry of Adam Kossowski and Michael Clark.

92

A good friend

Around this time the death of the farmer who occupied the dilapidated farmhouse and barns at the entrance to The Friars brought these buildings onto the market. They were bought by Reed's Paper Mill across the river. Malachy was concerned lest there would be industrial development of the property, blighting the entrance of The Friars. Fortunately, Mr. Sensenbrenner, an American director of Kimberly Clark Paper Mills, acted on behalf of the Carmelites vis-à-vis Reed's Paper Mill, enabling the Carmelites to purchase the property at a reasonable price. The Carmelites were lucky to have such a generous advocate as Mr. Sensenbrenner.

Over at Allington Castle generosity was not in the air. Major maintenance work had to be done, and despite lobbying by Lord Cornwallis, the Lord Lieutenant of Kent, and the local Member of Parliament, along with other public figures, no help was forthcoming from the Historic Building Council. Malachy could only wonder at the lack of vision in maintaining our heritage.

The iron gates at the entrance to the Relic Chapel.

93

Yet all the while, work was moving on steadily around the Shrine at Aylesford, with the sanctuary paved and the altar finished. Great iron gates had been made at a local forge, one for the Relic Chapel and the other for St. Anne's Chapel, at a cost of £500. Around this time the bank manager rang asking how much overdraft would be needed; Malachy's enigmatic reply was *"How should I know?!"*

The Feast of Our Lady of Mount Carmel on 16th July was always the highlight of the calendar for Malachy, but as the Shrine was (and still is) largely in the open air, celebrations were at the mercy of the elements. This was evident on a day in 1961; while the Mass with ordinations experienced gentle rain, it poured in the afternoon. Despite the inclement weather the pilgrims found shelter and at atmosphere of prayer. Bishop Cowderoy was deeply moved, and speaking to the crowd called Aylesford *"the Jewel of Southwark Diocese"*. He could only thank God for what had been achieved, and what was still being done.

Despite the weather, progress on the Shrine went ahead thanks to scores of voluntary workers from all over Europe. The main work was in the Sanctuary area of The Friars, and completing the Relic Chapel was a major focus. At the same time, developments at Allington were going ahead; more accommodation, as well as plans of turning the barn into a noble chapel, and a vision of 50 bedrooms for retreatants. Malachy took as his motto a text from Carmelite Evening Prayer: *"Give us the courage to build anew, quicken our desire to grow and increase, and grant us good success."*

In the midst of activity, Malachy was sensitive to the needs of people living alone. He thought about all the people who work hard but come home to a bleak flat. He hoped that such people would find a sense of communion through visits to Aylesford.

Portuguese interlude

In June 1961 Malachy went to Portugal for some sunshine. He made the journey by train, and observed in France scores of villages that were just as they had been a thousand years earlier. As the train groaned over the mountain gradients of Spain, however, Malachy

94

marvelled at the lack of settlements in the otherwise cultivated countryside. Malachy wondered at the wide views and the dust with the wind blowing from the Sierra Nevada mountains. Compared with Spain, Portugal seemed to be on a smaller scale; the train ran round small hills and gorges till it reached Porto (or Oporto as it is also known in English). The railway station was originally a monastery, and on one wall Malachy saw depicted the military general-turned-Carmelite lay brother Nuno Álvares Pereira (1360-1431) defeating the Spaniards. Nuno is a national hero in Portugal, and in 2009 was canonized for his life of prayer and poverty.

Painting of Saint Nuno created for his canonisation in 2009.

95

Malachy had family links with Porto, as a nun who helped run a large college for girls was a relative of his. He had stayed at the convent on a previous visit. Sister King was an Irishwoman in exile but loved all things Portuguese. She knew Lúcia Santos, one of the visionaries of Fátima, as they had been novices together in the Institute of the Sisters of Saint Dorothy, before Lúcia left to become a Carmelite. Malachy admired Sister King who was a big woman in every sense. Malachy always found tall women significant! He was also able to meet up with the English-speaking community in Porto and go to Fátima on a pilgrimage.

American journeys

As the summer of 1961 ended, Malachy was asked to go to the United States to appeal for Aylesford and spread the apostolate. Just before he left for the States he was able – with the help of the Sainte Union nuns – to set up a centre where young Irish girls could find friendship and support. This was to offer a vital meeting place, a chance to escape bleakness, and to find that you were not alone.

In the autumn Malachy took up the invitation of the North American Carmelites to come and make an appeal for Aylesford. The first thing he realised was the need of a schedule, so that his visit could be slotted into a proper timetable. Malachy was used to things happening, and yet in his life things often began to happen and come together by chance and good fortune.

Mary Mount College.

Malachy travelled by ship, a huge liner with 1,500 passengers. For Malachy the vessel seemed like a desert. On the whole conversations seemed to be most superficial, with the food on board being the main topic. Apart from a sun deck, the ship was enclosed and felt claustrophobic. Later in the voyage the ship ran into a hurricane which hardly perturbed Malachy.

New York and the sight of Carmelite confreres revived Malachy's spirit. His first assignment

96

was to stand in for the chaplain at Mary Mount College at Tarrytown. Mary Mount was a Liberal Arts College set in stunning countryside in the Hudson Valley. The sisters who ran the college were Irish with many links to the Carmelites. In his writing about the experience, Malachy admits the vision and energy of the sisters and – like many nuns he would meet – their commitment to women's education.

Malachy's next stop was the home of student friars in Middletown, in New York State's Orange County. From there he went to the Carmelite novitiate house at Thorvale Farm in Williamstown, Massachusetts, formerly home of the poet and Nobel laureate Sinclair Lewis. Thorvale Farm was a beautiful Georgian mansion with rolling acres of woodland, an ideal setting for a contemplative community.

A bonus for Malachy on his American visit was the fact that he knew the Carmelite Prior Provincial, Fr. Richard Nagle, as well as Fr. Lawrence Flanagan, a pioneer of the Order in the States, well over 80 years-old but tall and commanding. He remembered visiting Aylesford with Malachy in 1929, hoping it would one day be Carmelite again.

As Malachy travelled in the States, he was impressed by the parish school system, funded by the parishioners and staffed by teaching sisters. He gathered that there were around 170,000 sisters engaged in teaching, working in hospitals, and other ministries. It was arguably the heyday of the Catholic Church in North America, a Church that was largely of European origin: Irish, Poles, and Italians. The latter half of the 20th Century would see significant demographic changes.

Mount Carmel Spiritual Centre, Niagara Falls.

A highlight of Malachy's visit to upstate New York brought him into neighbouring Canada. Just by Niagara Falls was a college and high school for those preparing to become Carmelites. The Falls were awe-inspiring, but Malachy was most interested in sharing with the aspiring friars his vision of the apostolate at Aylesford.

97

Malachy realized that, thus far, he had only been on the eastern fringes of the American continent. After a while on the East Coast, Malachy was ready to travel into the West, to Kansas City. New York on one level fascinated him, but its towering buildings seemed to dwarf human beings and leave no room for companionship. Anyhow, Malachy had friends in Kansas City who wanted him to spend Christmas with them, and despite the snow Malachy reached his destination thanks to the skill of the pilot. Malachy received a warm welcome from Jolin and Dora Cunningham who had come to know Malachy when visiting Aylesford. The Cunninghams were generous and wealthy. Malachy was fascinated by their Afro-American servants and talked of them in a way which would be politically incorrect today. Despite the snow Malachy was able to visit a number of religious houses and was impressed by their vitality and their willingness to hear the story of Aylesford.

Downtown New Orleans in 1961.

His next stop was New Orleans where he had an invitation to talk from a group of Carmelite sisters. Again Malachy was amazed at the outreach and commitment of the sisters, and although the snow was left behind him, he was also aware of the fact that the whole area was subject to storms and flooding.

From the Gulf of Mexico the next stop was Houston in Texas, capital of the oil industry, and then to Tucson, Arizona, where in the desert

Left: Salpointe Catholic High School, Tucson, in 1953
Right: Santa Catalina Mountains overlooking Tuscon.

98

the Carmelites ran (as they still do) a school in a breath-taking setting, surrounded by jagged mountains that look as if they need finishing.

From Arizona Malachy made the relatively short journey to Los Angeles, which was recovering from storms and floods. It is a city of palms and every type of flowering tree, but what Malachy focussed  on was the name *Los Angeles* (Spanish for 'The Angels'). The name is linked to the 18th-Century Franciscan, Junípero Serra, the 'Apostle of California' who was canonised in 2015. Junípero evangelized the area along with his Franciscan confreres, and each settlement was given the name of a saint or an angel. Reflecting on Fra Junípero and angels, Malachy wrote *"an angel's mind is a whole world of pure knowledge."*

St. Raphael's Catholic Church in Los Angeles, served by the Carmelites since 1934.

In Los Angeles there was a good presence of Carmelite friars to encourage Malachy. In fact, two of them had been novices under Malachy's direction in 1930s, and they made sure he could appeal for Aylesford in their parish church. Malachy was impressed at the resourcefulness of young people working their way through college.

From the parish Malachy went to Crespi Carmelite High School at Encino near Hollywood. He found talk about Aylesford daunting as he faced some 800 young men at the college used to the *"hard sell"*.

Whilst Malachy was in Hollywood it was arranged that he should meet up with John Ford, the famous Irish-American film director well-known for many movies including *The Quiet Man*, for which he had won one of his four Best Director Oscars. Malachy found John Ford blunt, with a powerful personality and presence. It was clear that he was a generous man, but he already had his own charities to support. In fact, the whole visit had something surreal about it, considering that John Ford confided that he saw his fellow Hollywood stars as often empty. Indeed, for Malachy the whole environment of

John Ford with (right) actor Maureen O'Hara in the West of Ireland during filming of The Quiet Man in 1951.

Hollywood seemed absurd. Malachy headed back East, calling on the Cunninghams in Kansas, before heading north to Chicago, and then back to England. He had been away from England more than six months, keeping to a gruelling schedule, and impressed by the vitality of the American Church as well as the welcome he received from fellow Carmelites.

Second Vatican Council

Pope John XXIII and his calling of the Second Vatican Council, to begin in October 1962, held Malachy's attention. Pope John was a disconcerting contrast to Pope Pius XII. Pius was an aristocrat, tall and frail, seemingly remote; it seemed that he would be the last great pope. Pope John, on the other hand, was from farming stock north of Bergamo. Malachy saw the pope as literally down to earth; in the end he was an old man with the vigour and vision of youth. He understood that the Church is not a museum. John saw himself in the hands of the Lord, and so he felt he was in good hands. Malachy hoped that the Council would bring a quickening and an awakening to the Church. He felt it would be a time of

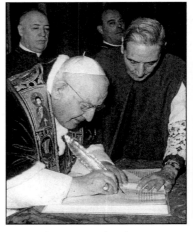

Pope (now Saint) John XXIII signing the edict convoking the Second Vatican Council.

100

renewal, and a time for the medicine of mercy not condemnation. He saw the need for the Holy Spirit to fill hearts with love.

The bishops of the Church gathered in St. Peter's during the Second Vatican Council.

Besides Pope John's hopes for a helpful outcome to the Council, there was the Cuban Missile Crisis to worry about. The stand-off between the Russians and Americans was serious enough to threaten nuclear war; fortunately, brinkmanship gave way to diplomacy in the end, and the fear of widespread death was lifted.

Despite Malachy's extensive travels in the United States, he did not bring back to Kent much more than $8,000. The bank overdraft was creeping up again.

Vicente Ballister, the last Spanish stone mason at Aylesford, polishing the ceramics of Adam Kossowski in the Relic Chapel.

The building work at Aylesford was progressing bit by bit. Workshops were finished, but the Main Shrine and the two large chapels adjoining it – the Relic Chapel and St. Joseph Chapel – were incomplete. The open-air sanctuary around the Main Shrine was still awaiting two large ceramic depictions of archangels. The task ahead could seem almost impossible; the fog

101

Adam Kossowski's 'Angel of Aylesford' towers protectively over the Main Shrine.

that Malachy describes at Allington could be a metaphor for his difficulty in seeing the way forward.

A cold castle but a warm welcome

The castle at Allington was Malachy's home, and it proved to be bitterly cold in the winter months, leaving him prey to flu and a feeling that the very marrow of his bones was frozen by the cruel northeast wind. When the hard winter finally – if reluctantly – ended, signs of spring lifted Malachy's head. He took delight in the rivalry of the thrush and blackbird competing for the late worms. Finding a copy of Saint Patrick's *Confession* gave Malachy insights into the life of the Apostle of Ireland. In writing Malachy pointed out the cruelty of the marauders who took Patrick captive, but then put Patrick in his context of a time of radical change. Malachy conceded that Patrick was not a great intellectual like his contemporary Augustine of Hippo, but was nevertheless a man who trusted in God's presence. Of Patrick's great prayer *The Breastplate*, Malachy writes: *"This prayer is Patrick – if the whole man could be a prayer, could any prayer be more strong or terrible?"*

Spring in 1963 came too slowly. May was a cold month, only redeemed by the song of blackbirds. Malachy went back to Ireland to be present when a niece was professed as a Brigidine Sister at Tullow in County Carlow. Describing the town, Malachy mentions that *"it narrowly escaped being a village"*. The spire of the parish church gives the town its status; a sharp pointer to heaven and the first Catholic Church to be built with a spire since Penal Days.

102

The convent of the Brigidine Sisters in Tullow, photographed in 2013.

Whenever Malachy was back in Ireland he connected to the innate poetry of the people, in this case a farmer who was a relative by marriage: *"He spoke as men under heaven should speak – beautiful Wicklow speak."*

Back at Allington, Malachy was able to welcome Archbishop Alberto Castelli, Secretary to the Italian Bishops. The archbishop was a great enthusiast for the works of G. K. Chesterton and Hilaire Belloc, having translated their writings into Italian. In fact, his reason for visiting England was to visit Belloc's relatives, the Jebbs. He was also delighted to meet Archie Colquhoun, who had translated Alessandro Manzoni's great Italian novel *I Promessi Sposi* into English as *The Betrothed*. Archbishop Castelli also delighted Malachy by taking his Scapular devotion prayer – *"Use me today"* – and rendering it into Italian: *"Usami Oggi."*

Aylesford Priory meant a great deal to the Bishop of Southwark, Cyril Cowderoy. He liked coming to pray and find peace. The little Chapel of Saint Anne just off the Main Shrine was dedicated in 1962 to the memory of his mother Anne. The dedication was a great consolation to the bishop on the loss of his mother, as well as a tribute to Adam Kossowski's work in ceramics and scraffito frescos. These set-off the beauty of a 15th-Century 'Anna selbsdritt' statue from the Continent showing Saint Anne carrying her

The Saint Anne Chapel at Aylesford Priory.

daughter Mary and grandson Jesus, both as infants.

103

Saint Anne is depicted in the chapel at Aylesford in (left) ceramic by Adam Kossowski, and (right) a Renaissance statue.

One afternoon at Aylesford a group of children were gazing up at the statue of Our Lady in the Main Shrine, and when asked for their opinion about the artwork their response was "*We think she is terrific!*"

Malachy wrote "*I thought of the great rivers of children who swept through Aylesford last year on the way to the summer of their lives.*"

Malachy also spoke eloquently of Pope John, having heard that the pontiff was dying. In Malachy's opinion Pope John came to bring life to a dying age; a new Church, a new World was being born of his charity and humility.

Malachy with a young pilgrim.

One of Malachy's traits was to be either an enthusiast or dismissive. He was a great admirer of the writers Alessandro Manzoni and Paul Claudel. Claudel was poet, philosopher and mystic; his play *The Satin Slipper* could be compared to the work of Dante. However, Malachy dismissed contemporary fiction as reading like an overdue confession. He dismissed Graham Greene as writing to a formula, stating that his novels were well constructed but he reads as a skeleton.

104

Alessandro Manzoni (left) and Paul Claudel, two Catholic writers of whom Fr. Malachy approved greatly.

Malachy always had an eye for beauty in nature, and never allowed the glory of it to be lost. The sight of the Lombardy poplars at Allington in autumn leaf and evening light made him think of angels and archangels filling the space between earth and sky.

The saints are alive

In a similar vein Malachy had a great sense of the vitality of the saints. He speaks of Teresa of Avila gate-crashing his thoughts. Her awakening to God thrilled Malachy, her dissatisfaction with her past, her sense of mediocrity. He saw her nobility and grace perfecting her nature. A born writer, with her discerning candour Teresa understood the human soul and the light of the spirit. Contemplatives are the great explorers of the human spirit; they are in love with God.

Just as Malachy was writing about contemplation, the Second Vatican Council was underway, and it encouraged Malachy to have unity weekends at Allington Castle, bringing together Christians from various backgrounds. This was a new venture and a creative outreach.

John F. Kennedy's assassination in November 1963 caused Malachy to ponder on the Irish Diaspora, and to see in the late American President the line of blood; tracing ancestry and being proud of family names.

105

Pilgrimage

Easter 1964 saw Malachy embarking on an ecumenical pilgrimage to the Mediterranean and Holy Land. For him it was a wrench to leave Allington and its springtime beauty. He affirms in his writings that Allington and Aylesford absorb him with no time for radio, television, or newspapers, and little interest in small talk. In Malachy's estimation life is too short for trivia; what matters is silence, and what is beyond silence. The pilgrimage was therefore a challenge to engage Malachy, and see what registered with him. His comments on Islam show an interest in the Sufi movement, the mystical Islamic belief and practice in which Muslims seek to find the truth of divine love and knowledge through direct personal experience of God. Malachy regarded Sufism as the possible 'saving' of Islam, taking away what he considered to be its savage drive, but it was not to be; Malachy saw in Islam a certain cruel loneliness.

In Malta, Miss Mable Strickland gave hospitality to the pilgrims and showed the beautiful churches built by the Knights of Saint John, but in Malachy's view Malta is most famous for its association with Saint Paul, shipwrecked there on his way to Rome.

In Valletta, Malta's capital, the dome of the Carmelite Basilica and the spire of the Anglican Cathedral stand side-by-side.

106

Before reaching the Holy Land, Malachy travelled through Lebanon and Syria, and his view of the wide-open country and peaceful villages stands in sharp contrast to the destruction that has taken place there in the second decade of the Twenty-First Century, and to the tensions that now exist in the Middle East.

One of Malachy's pre-occupations in the Holy Land was finding churches dedicated to Elijah (or Elias) the prophet, revered by Carmelites as spiritual father of the Order. Malachy was conscious of the tensions between the Arab population and the new state of Israel. He sensed an uneasy truce, and also saw desolation and division.

If anything moved him it was Ephesus in Turkey: its amazing ruins; its links with Saint Paul; with the great Council of 431 that called Mary

Mergem Ana Evi, or 'Mother Mary's House' near Ephesus is the site Catholic Christians believe to be where Our Lady lived with Saint John.

Theotokos ('God-bearer'); and the tradition that Mary came to Ephesus with the beloved disciple and spent her last years there. The House of Mary is some distance from Ephesus; it is a wonderful place of peace and prayer, regarded as a holy site by both Christians and Muslims.

The pilgrimage lasted a month, and so Malachy was back at Aylesford for ordinations in July and the translation of Saint Simon Stock's relic to its new home in the newly built Relic Chapel.

About this time there was a significant Anglican pilgrimage to Aylesford. This was a pilgrimage of reparations for the excessive destruction that took place during the Reformation, and a reminder of the growing devotion to Mary in the Anglican Communion. Malachy believed that devotion to Our Lady in the Church of England owed much to Walsingham, a major site of medieval pilgrimage destroyed at the Reformation, but restored by both Anglicans and Catholics in

107

the Twentieth Century. Though the restored practice of pilgrimage to Walsingham has at times faced hostility within the Church of England, it is in continuity with a long tradition of English Marian devotion.

The 'Holy House' in the Anglican Shrine at Walsingham, established in 1931.

Later in the year Malachy was wracked by sciatica, getting no help from medication nor much attention from the hospital consultant, but admiring the commitment of the nurses. It was nearly Christmas before the pain had eased. During this time, Malchy read a collection of essays written by Pope Paul VI when Archbishop of Milan. Malachy found the pope's writings positive, and very much of the spirit of Vatican II which was coming to a close. The essays were translated by Archie Colquhoun, and the translation (the last work Archie was to do) did justice to the original.

Memories of youth

As Malachy grew older, his mind turned back to memories of his childhood. Like many of his generation, Malachy was proud of being a Wicklow man, and proud of his roots in the country. The sea was not far from his birth place, and as a boy he had loved the tall ships and the ways of the fishermen. The coastal town of Arklow had a family member running a hotel that Malachy reckoned to be *"quiet and gracious."*

108

Another memory was the chapel at Askanagap where the family – thirteen children, nine boys – had gone to Mass. The congregation was mainly mountain people, smallholders. One of the smallholders, Pat, was sacristan, helped by Mrs. Travers who gave the priest his breakfast of tea, toast, and boiled eggs. The priest rode over from the parish house five miles away, and Malachy recalls: *"The Priest cared for his horse more than himself. An idyllic world, and it produced three outstanding friars."*

Another episode Malachy recalled from the past was linked to Faversham in 1927 when he was parish priest. He was somewhat disconsolate; the parish was almost petering out with only about 30 practising Catholics, so Malachy went on the lookout for the lapsed. Malachy found an old man in a pub garden who had been at sea and had drifted away from the Church. The old man said he had something that had been given him by a priest in Melbourne. The something was a Carmelite scapular, and the priest had been a Carmelite friar. Malachy was able to help the old man make his peace and join the Catholic congregation in Plantation Road. The old man died soon after his reconciliation.

A sign of getting old is vividly recalling the past as it becomes a golden age. A visit from an old friend, Catrin Daniels, prompted Malachy to reminisce about his years in Wales. They had been arduous, but the friendships made then were life-giving. Catrin and her husband Professor Daniels were passionate about all things Welsh. Catrin was a poet in Welsh and English, and helped to energise Y Cylch Catholig ('The Catholic Circle'), an organisation for Welsh-speaking Catholics. Later on the Carmelite friars John and Gregory FitzGerald would do much to promote Welsh in the life of the Church. Likewise, Mrs. Wynne, who enabled the Catholic church at Lampeter to be built, was committed to Welsh culture and to supporting the church in a practical way, being its custodian when a priest was unable to be in residence. Malachy had a pithy saying about the Reformation in these islands: *"The Irish lost the language and kept the faith, while the Welsh kept the language and lost the faith."* Access to the Bible in Welsh was crucial for the course of religion in Wales from the 18th Century onwards.

Dedication of the Shrine at Aylesford

July 1965 saw the solemn dedication of the Shrine at Aylesford. There were three days of celebrations, attended by the Carmelite Prior General, Cardinal John Carmel Heenan, Cyril Cowderoy (raised earlier that year from Bishop to Archbishop of Southwark), and an Italian Carmelite bishop, Telesforo Giovanni Cioli.

Bishop Telesforo Giovanni Cioli, an Italian Carmelite, consecrating the Relic Chapel altar at Aylesford Priory in July 1965. He is assisted by Carmelite friars Bro. Nuno Benito and Fr. Andrew Donnelly.

The Relic Chapel takes its name from the relic of Saint Simon Stock, housed in a reliquary designed by Adam Kossowski that represents the hermits' cells on Mount Carmel.

110

The dedication of the Main Shrine to the Assumption of the Glorious Virgin Mary on 18ᵗʰ July 1965.

Carmelite friars praying their traditional 'Saturday Station' at the Main Shrine in 2007.

111

Cardinal Heenan at the consecration of the altars and rededication of the Shrine.

Aerial view of the Main Shrine, chapels and piazza at The Friars.

The dedication festivities were a time for Malachy to reflect on all that had happened since he had first seen The Friars in 1929, when it was still the home of the Hewitt family. Mrs. Hewitt had loved the place, and Malachy was sure she would have been pleased to know it was again in Carmelite hands. Again, Malachy reflected that he had come to Aylesford in faith, uprooting himself after 13 years in Wales, but he realised that it was the poor widows giving of their savings who enabled the dedication to take place. It all happened so wonderfully swiftly.

112

The summer of 1965 also saw the ordination of some Carmelite friars. At the time of writing this biography, one of them – Pat O'Keeffe – is still active today in school chaplaincy. The other was called Simon Stock, and the fact that someone with the same name as a famous Carmelite saint should be a friar caused more than a ripple of interest.

It is interesting that, writing in 1965, Malachy endorses the "*new liturgy*" brought in by the Second Vatican Council. He believed that the use of the vernacular would help people recognise the gestures and symbolism of the Mass, and mean their prayer more deeply. He recognised the shortcomings of the Roman Rite, and that renewal has always been the way of the Church. His writings also demonstrate that he had been studying the course of liturgical renewal, recognising the valuable work done by the Benedictines at St. John's Abbey in Collegeville, Minnesota. Malachy saw liturgical reform taking Christians back to the spirit of the Early Church.

Family ties were important to Malachy, and up and down Ireland he had cousins, nephews and nieces. A family that gave generous support were the Scallons. They lived over the Northern Irish border in Fermanagh, and proved generous helpers to Aylesford. He was fond of his nephews Sean and Seamus Lynch, who were starting a career as farmers, bringing the land back to fertility. He enjoyed family weddings, and described people with disarming comments: "*The mother was there – looking young and fresh – a necessary and beloved presence.*"

Serious illness

With the celebrations over, Malachy was taken ill out of the blue with a bleeding ulcer that required blood transfusions and convalescence. Hospital seemed like another planet as he settled into life on a ward with 13 other patients. Malachy admired the dedication of the nurses, but felt there was something too clinical in the care. He found great solace in praying the Rosary, feeling eased by the rhythm of the prayers. Visiting hours were seen by Malachy as a time of love, when families came transforming the wards with their care and gentle concern. All in all, Malachy was aware in hospital of being in a new world that knew little of the world of Aylesford.

113

1965 was a year of contrasts: from celebrations to illness and floods. The floods in December caused immense damage, killing off the poultry, wrecking the newsletter office, and putting the laundry out of action. Malachy felt sorry for the Prior, Richard Hearne, who had just succeeded Fr. Kilian. However, with generous help much of the damage was repaired.

End of the Second Vatican Council

1965 also saw the end of the Second Vatican Council, and Malachy was trying to fathom its outcome. Influenced by Yves Congar (a French Dominican friar whose theology was very influential at the Council), Malachy began to see the role of the bishop as lived out in the Early Church as fundamental to its life, and the need for a simpler way of expressing that role today. Congar also saw, in keeping with that role, an end to elaborate dress for bishops. In place of opulent robes, Malachy was more impressed by the simple white cassock in which Pope Paul VI – a fragile and holy figure – addressed the United Nations. Malachy also liked the thrust of service behind Saint Augustine's motto: *"I am a bishop for you."*

Pope Paul VI addressing the United Nations Organisation in New York, October 1965.

114

One major outcome of the Council was that ecumenical dialogue between Christians of different denominations was endorsed as a positive way forward for Catholics. Malachy was delighted that Anglican pilgrimage groups came to Aylesford. "*We are all Christians*", he wrote, believing that those who were not against the Carmelites were with the Carmelites. An Anglican clergyman, Dr. Box, the Rector of Bexhill, was a generous donor who contributed to the decoration of the Relic Chapel. In many ways the template for Catholicism in Malachy's eyes was the faith of the Irish, which seemed to him to be in marked contrast to the English practice of religion. It would be interesting to know what Malachy's comments would be on the Catholic and other Churches in Ireland in these opening years of the Twenty First Century.

Collaborators in ministry

A man called Percy Kitchen had been a crucial presence in the restoration of The Friars as a Carmelite community. He had a rough exterior, but was a devoted worker. Percy was able to organise and train the other workers, and was invaluable at translating the architect's drawings into the finished work. Percy found faith as he worked at the shrine, and his work is – in its essence – imprinted on the restoration efforts at Aylesford. When Percy Kitchen died in the mid-1960s, the loss touched Malachy strongly.

Another loss to Aylesford was Betty Chapman. Betty was Jewish by origin, but had spent many years searching for her spiritual home. She found her way to Catholicism when she was in hospital, and at about the same time her husband likewise found faith as a Catholic. Betty became a member of the Carmelite Third Order, and with other helpers founded Aylesford Tours and Pilgrimages, bringing thousands of pilgrims by coach from London to Aylesford and Allington. The first pastoral task I undertook after ordination was to go to Lourdes as chaplain to a group Betty had organised. I found her kind, and tolerant, and an excellent teacher in helping me with my ministry. Sadly, Betty died in 1966 after a severe illness, but she accepted her ailment with gentle faith. Malachy was conscious of her family's grief. Generous helpers like Betty did much to promote Aylesford,

115

and with the *Pilgrims' Newsletter* reaching 75,000 subscribers, the apostolate was significant.

Malachy was very conscious of how many people in Britain were ceasing to believe in a personal God. Through the *Pilgrims' Newsletter* he asked his readers to bear witness to the truth, and remove obstacles and prejudices in matters of faith.

Even though Vatican II had endorsed devotion to Our Lady, in the years afterwards Malachy felt that the Rosary was diminishing in popularity as a devotion. He saw the Rosary as an essential element of the prayer life at Aylesford, with its processions around the Rosary Way. Alongside devotion to the Rosary, in Malachy's mind the Carmelite Brown Scapular figured equal in importance, which he promoted through his *"Use me today"* apostolate. Malachy was right in his worries about devotion, and for a while there was indeed a falling off in popular piety, but in recent times new generations have discovered the Rosary as a form of meditative prayer rooted in the Scriptures, and the Scapular is being reclaimed as a sign of service and belonging within the Carmelite Family, under the protective care of Mary.

A procession at Aylesford Priory in 2007.

116

*A Carmelite friar enrolling Aylesford pilgrims in the
Brown Scapular Confraternity in 2006.*

Renewal

Writing the *Pilgrims' Newsletter* in February 1967, Malachy was aware
that many of his readers were upset by aspects of the renewal flowing
from the Second Vatican Council. Though he embraced the liturgical
changes, he was right to point out that many were carried out without
enough explanation to churchgoers. Also, some enthusiasts were
insensitive in the way they carried out renewal, stripping churches
of artwork in a desire to simplify the style of worship. He points to
the piety of Orthodox Christians with their reverence of icons, seeing
the space inside a church building as a representation of heaven.
Bareness and bleakness can result from a mistaken fear of idolatry.

Malachy tried to remind his readers that Mass in the vernacular was
meant to enable fuller participation in the celebration by God's
people. Yet change without explanation or consultation was no
help to renewal. Of course, liturgical modifications continue to
cause controversy to this day. The new translation of the Roman
Missal introduced in English-speaking countries in 2011 has caused
controversy with its archaic language, and again there is a widespread
sense that the people of God have not been part of the project.

117

In the August 1967 *Pilgrims' Newsletter*, Malachy records an encounter with the writer G. K. Chesterton and his wife. Malachy was on the same train as them, and by chance stayed at the same hotel. Malachy recalls meeting up with G. K. later in the evening: *"He was a great bulky man, tall and graceful in his movements."* Malachy treasured their conversation which ranged over a wide spectrum. G. K. saw Hilaire Belloc and himself as soldiers on the ramparts, defending the city that had no time to find meaning. He spoke of Teresa of Avila and other saints with intrinsic knowledge. For Malachy that one meeting was a memory to treasure.

G. K. Chesterton (left) and Hilaire Belloc, two widely-respected Catholic authors of Twentieth-Century Britain.

Malachy was open to ecumenical relations and valued the presence and support of Anglicans. Allington Castle proved to be a popular

venue for inter-church and inter-faith meetings. Among participants was the Russian Orthodox Archbishop Anthony Bloom (Metropolitan Anthony of Sourozh), a great teacher on prayer; in him Malachy found a soul-fellow. Also among the group there was a Buddhist Abbot, a refugee from Tibet. Malachy found him to be a truly saintly man, innocence personified and yet most intelligent, a person of prayer who valued the hospitality of Catholic monasteries and friaries.

Metropolitan Anthony Bloom.

118

While being involved in the contemporary, Malachy also had a vivid sense of the past. Looking back on his days in Faversham reminded him of the workhouse and its bleakness. He went on a sick call to the workhouse and found an old Irishman, a man of the road, dying. The notice by the bed said "No friends". Malachy was sad that such a man of great dignity should be so alone and dying in the bleakness of the institution. Malachy officiated at the funeral; he was the sole mourner.

Malachy and Carmelite brethren eating in the small community refectory at Aylesford Priory.

Father Elias

Portrait of Fr. Elias Lynch by Bernard Leigh, at the National Shrine of Saint Jude, Faversham.

Malachy's older brother and fellow Carmelite died in November 1967. Elias was an Institution. For Malachy his brother was so original and many-sided. Chief of his virtues was his great-heartedness. He had immense vision and could never do a small thing. He was an original, and also had no successor. Malachy marvelled at Elias' business acumen, and his ability to take on so many roles in Faversham: town councillor; air raid warden; a good unconventional preacher; and a great conversationalist. As novelist Kate O'Brien said, "How proudly he loved the Carmelite Order and all it stood for".

119

Time of change

Writing in the summer of 1968, Malachy was shocked by the assassination of Robert Kennedy in the United States. He saw Kennedy as a figure of hope for a younger generation, since he believed that the politician cared for the poor and for race relations. How can we make sense of such random violence?!

The papal encyclical *Humanae Vitae* was promulgated in August 1968. Malachy noted with sadness the hostility against the teaching's reception. He saw contraception as lowering the dignity of women and being against civilisation. It was clear that Malachy was firmly behind the pope, and bewildered at the lack of positive response, especially from many Catholics and some Catholic journals. Little did Malachy realise how much of a watershed moment the response to the pope's letter would prove to be; some 50 years later the issues are still live in the Church.

Malachy in the Cloisters at The Friars.

120

A time of change in the Church also marked a time of change for Malachy. Ill health and decisions made about development at Allington put an end to an important chapter in his life. The plans to build a 'City of Mary' there were put on hold. Some accommodation had been built, and the great tithe barn was re-roofed with peg tiles. That project was carried out by Roger Brown, a gifted builder who had worked on the shrine at Aylesford. Roger, a member of the Carmelite Third Order, dedicated many years to maintaining the fabric of the Castle. However, the main building project was shelved. Malachy was desperately disappointed, and felt small-mindedness was behind the decision. In his mind's eye he felt that the Prior of Aylesford was to blame. Allied to this decision was a marked decline in Malachy's health, as his mobility became more and more difficult. He needed assistance to walk any distance, but thankfully there were willing helpers. Sheila Blaxter, who lived in Pine Cottage in the Castle grounds, was a loyal friend. She ensured that Malachy was able to go over to Aylesford every afternoon to say the Rosary and meet pilgrims, and for him this was an important lifeline. Over the last few years of Malachy's life, many members of the Carmelite Third Order showed him great care, and the lay community at the Castle saw to his daily needs.

Thanks to the hard work of Malachy and others, the 'mission' to re-establish the Carmelite friars in Britain had grown to such an extent that in 1969 the communities were granted autonomy within the Order. The newly-erected Anglo-Welsh Province of Carmelites held its first Chapter (meeting of the brothers), electing a leadership team to guide the new jurisdiction. The event gave Malachy great hope. The Castle was also becoming more integrated into the life of the Province, with a Carmelite becoming the Warden and the Vocations Director, making the Castle the base for his work. The changes involved in building good relationships between Malachy and the younger friars were not always easy to manage; they required a blend of poetry and pragmatism. Despite illness, Malachy kept up the apostolate of the *Pilgrims' Newsletter* at Aylesford, and a steady flow of visitors there and at Allington kept him involved in ministry and able to help people with prayer and a vision of life. Malachy was able to share meals with retreatants and conference participants;

121

conversation was as vital as the food. The groups that visited the Castle brought a special stimulus, especially the Society of Catholic Artists.

Malachy in his later years.

Lourdes

In the early summer of 1971 Malachy was able to go on pilgrimage to Lourdes again. The journey was made difficult by storms, and then to crown it all the hotel was closed as there had been a confusion with booking. When the pilgrims got into the hotel it was very cold as the heating had been turned off. Problems were soon forgotten as Malachy found peace in the prayerfulness of Lourdes: "*You see what love is and what love does.*" Malachy was able to concelebrate Mass each day and was taken to the healing waters of the baths on three occasions. Malachy was also able to visit the monastery of Carmelite nuns overlooking the Grotto, helped by Brother Michael who enabled him to get around in a wheelchair. Malachy found the

122

Prioress of the Carmel a strong personality very much *"alive"*. On the way out the sisters provided delicious biscuits and cordial, which Malachy thought a lovely gesture: *"Courtesy is the sister of charity."* The pilgrimage was life-enhancing, even though the flight back had fraught moments with one of the engines giving up. Despite such problems, we pilgrims were all hardly back home when another pilgrimage was being planned for late in the summer of 1972.

The interior of the chapel at Lourdes Carmel in 2015.

From the *Pilgrims' Newsletter* it is amazing to see how much Malachy was involved with and aware of the pilgrimages at Aylesford. Despite ill health he had amazing mental energy.

Malachy greets pilgrims from his car.

He makes generous comments about the modified habits that the sisters were wearing since Vatican II: *"they had got rid of the bulk and awkward extravagances."*

The Pilgrimage of the Sick on 15th August 1971 made Aylesford into a little Lourdes for the day, and to Malachy's delight the presiding bishop at the Eucharist, Daniel Mullins, had been a student at Aberystwyth when Malachy was Prior. He was pleased the sick and disabled were being made welcome at Aylesford, and access being made possible for all. He also linked the Sick Pilgrimage to the feast of the day, the Assumption, when Mary is particularly a sign of hope and comfort.

123

Young people

From 1969 onwards the Carmelites' apostolate at Allington took on a new emphasis as young people in particular were welcomed. The Castle took on the role of providing a pastoral centre for the youth of Southwark Archdiocese, with retreats, courses, and work promoting vocations. Besides this outreach, the Castle became a venue for music performances and other cultural activities. One event that impressed Malachy was a production of Shakespeare's *As You Like It*. It was played on the banks of the moat, with the Castle as the backdrop. Malachy was delighted with the production, and with Harriet who combined playing Rosalind with helping in the running of the Castle. The Great Hall was an excellent venue for Tudor and Renaissance music, and on Sundays it became a chapel where local Catholics gathered for Mass. It also delighted the groups of young people who gathered there to tell stories around the log fire. All of this needed help, and a whole team emerged with Biddy McNay looking after the housekeeping, Molly McLean seeing to the catering and finance, and Joan and Frieda Swingler from The Leaven Secular Institute. In addition, Vicente and Roger cared for the grounds and the fabric. Again, voluntary workers did much to care for the Castle with their generous help.

Fr. Malachy and the author (left) with young pilgrims.

124

Malachy during a school pilgrimage to The Friars.

While the constant coming and going of groups could be stressful, Malachy was pleased to see the vitality of the place and enjoyed contact with the young people. Besides the groups at Allington, there were individual retreatants who found help from time spent with Malachy. Despite ill health, his day was carefully structured with Mass around nine o'clock, then work on correspondence and writing the *Pilgrims' Newsletter* for Aylesford which was always rich in his wisdom. Malachy had a loyal secretary in Margaret Arkell who worked with him for many years. The afternoon saw him over in Aylesford and, like lunch, he would eat supper with a visiting group and his fellow friars. The time in between was given to prayer and an amazing amount of reading. Malachy had a universal mind when it came to reading matter, with a definite preference for Catholic writers. He loved Teresa of Avila and Julian of Norwich, Thomas Merton, Charles Peguy, Paul Claudel, G. K. Chesterton, Hilaire Belloc, Anthony Bloom, and Paul VI. One interesting author whom Malachy admired was Shushaku Endo, a Japanese writer who in his novels told of the persecution of Christians in the 17th Century. Endo was able to depict the Japanese psyche.

Despite such a full day, Malachy could feel lonely, declaring *"I'm marooned!"* Malachy needed to be with interesting and challenging people, and it was fascinating to see how absorbed he could become, drinking in the conversation. It gave him vitality – life.

His last newsletter

The last *Pilgrims' Newsletter* Malachy wrote was number 113. It came out in the spring of 1972, and Malachy begins by reminiscing about his time in Kinsale in the 1930s. He was intrigued by the parish priest

125

– *"the Venerable the Archdeacon"* – a title not to be questioned but rather to be accepted. The priest was old-fashioned even for that era; an institution in his Topper, but strangely anonymous.

Malachy had a great friend in Kinsale in Fr. McSwiney. This priest had been a lecturer in the seminary, but for various reasons – perhaps politics – he was appointed to Kinsale. Malachy found a soul-friend in this cultured, gifted, and visionary person. The two of them became firm friends and they would go for a long walk into the country discussing all manner of things. Sometimes they were joined by an ex-Jesuit who was a Celtic scholar and who enriched the conversation. Another of Fr. McSwiney's friends was Professor Fleischman who was in charge of the Cathedral Choir in Cork. According to Arnold Bax, the composer, the choir was the finest in Europe. The professor helped Malachy widen his appreciation of music, especially Palestrina, and Malachy passed on his enthusiasm for music to the novices. Father McSwiney died relatively young, fulfilling the saying "the good never grow old".

Titus reading.

A major part of that final newsletter is given over to memories of Titus Brandsma, the Dutch Carmelite friar martyred in Dachau. Malachy first met Titus when returning from a meeting for novice masters in Rome in 1934. Malachy was aware of the depth of faith in Titus' family, and their down-to-earth belief. Titus' father would light up his pipe and offer incense to God!

The Dutch Carmelites had a very conservative tradition, against which Titus could sometimes clash; he was against austerity for its own sake, inspired more by his down-to-earth Frisian background, warm family life, and wish to do good. Malachy was able to know Titus more fully when he stayed in Kinsale in 1935. Titus saw visiting

126

the sick as a priority, and Malachy was able to help the Dutchman with preparing the lectures he was to give in the States.

Malachy saw Titus as a generous spirit rising above the structures of what, at times, were rigorous expressions of religious life. Malachy admired Titus' generosity of spirit; the Dutchman would put himself out for anybody, and he was not just focussed on the purely academic. Even at the end, in the hospital in Dachau, Titus was praying for the nurse who was killing him by lethal injection. Titus always lived in the presence of God. Malachy wondered what it would have been like if Titus and the medieval English mystic Julian of Norwich could have met, and Titus would have translated her teaching. Drawing on one of Dame Julian's most famous images, both she and Titus would have known the Who of Creation in a hazelnut.

As we remarked earlier, through the good offices of Leonard Cheshire, Malachy came on a prayer vigil to Dachau and went to see the horror of the place and hear the testimony of survivors. He could see how the suffering had broken so many. It is said that at least 2,000 clergy were imprisoned and made to do forced labour, growing herbs to be used as medicine for wounded German airmen. There are stories of Eucharistic hosts being smuggled into the camp so that those incarcerated could have the Sacrament; at least there was some underground of care.

Besides memories making up the heart of Malachy's last *Pilgrims' Newsletter*, there is a section that shows him to have been a keen observer of the natural world. It is the rollcall of birds that he could observe from his room in the Castle courtyard. His constant visitor was a blackbird, while a beautiful thrush comes to his door. On the moat bank there are swans, ducks and moorhens. A family of blue tits live in a crevice in the stonework, and all these creatures are fed by the housekeeper Biddy. The visitor Malachy particularly welcomes is the kingfisher, with its electric blue plumage, hovering and diving much to Malachy's delight. These were the joys of the last spring of his life.

127

Malachy at prayer.

Last days

By Easter of 1972 Malachy was frail and worn out. Since his days in Faversham he had been totally committed to ministry and his life as a Carmelite. For a big man he was at times both frail and vulnerable, with sciatica and diabetes as constant companions.

With the years he became less mobile, prone to infections, and needing more care. He became quite ill on Holy Saturday, but he rallied after receiving the Sacrament of the Sick and was able to pay a final visit to Aylesford. While he had become very weak physically, his mind was clear and he was able to take an interest in the Provincial Chapter that was taking place at the Castle. He had asked readers of the *Newsletter* for prayers for the Chapter's outcome, and hoped to talk about it in the next edition. In the days up to his death on 5th May, Malachy was able to celebrate Mass most days, helped by his brother Fr. Kilian who was with him when he died. In those last weeks Malachy was lovingly cared for by devoted friends and his Carmelite brothers.

128

Funeral

Malachy's funeral was fittingly held at the Main Shrine in Aylesford Priory, with Archbishop Cyril Cowderoy presiding, and attended by many Carmelite friars, sisters, and Lay Carmelites, including members of The Leaven. During the Mass, just after the consecration, the heavens opened and there was a rush for shelter. The one person who stayed in place was the Archbishop who remained at his prie-dieu out of respect until the rain stopped and Mass was resumed; he explained that he could not have left Malachy's mortal remains unguarded.

Father Malachy's funeral.

Fr. Malachy's grave marker in the cemetery at The Friars. He is buried alongside the author's uncle, Brother Anthony McGreal.

129

Carmelite friar Fr. Edward Maguire gave the homily, and was able to point out the essence of the man. He said that Saint Paul's words could well be applied to Malachy: never grow tired of doing what is right. This was the hallmark of the man. Malachy never grew tired – perhaps those who worked with him did – but he always drove himself first. He achieved so much by finding artists who could speak of the spiritual in an open way. He created a space that was welcoming to all for whom goodness, truth, and beauty mattered. Edward asked the question: What sort of man was Malachy? And gave the answer: a combination of a medieval mystic and a renaissance prince, with vision and single mindedness, drive and determination. Difficulties never daunted him, and he saw himself as an instrument of Our Lady and God. Malachy had courage to undertake the restoration of Aylesford in difficult days, still very much post-war. He worked until he could give no more, but he attracted young and old with his great personal magnetism. Malachy's devotion to Our Lady was profound, and he saw her as one who could heal divisions among Christians.

Fr. Edward Maguire in 1976, then Carmelite Provincial, with Archbishop Cyril Cowderoy, in the Long Gallery at Allington Castle on the occasion of the Silver Jubilee of the Castle as a Carmelite community.

130

If anything defined Malachy it was his faith – his conviction. He was a visionary not always easy to live with. Malachy, in his turn, did not always feel that his Carmelite confreres were with him, perhaps because Malachy stood for what was challenging and different. The vision was accepted, but sometimes the question was how the vision could be achieved. To borrow from Yeats: "*Tread softly because you tread on my dreams.*" Wherever you tread in Aylesford, you tread on Malachy's dreams, but thank God he had courage to build anew.

Malachy made Aylesford a home for his Carmelite brothers, such as (left) Tommy Gallagher and Pat Geary, here celebrating their Diamond Jubilees of priesthood in 1991.

The Great Courtyard at The Friars, Aylesford, photographed in 2007.

131

Afterword

Among those attending Malachy's funeral in May 1972 was a twenty-eight year-old organist, John Tavener, who would go on to become widely-regarded as Britain's leading choral composer. Raised a Presbyterian, Tavener felt spiritually unfulfilled in that tradition. At the age of twelve he met Fr. Malachy, whom he described as *"one of the most interesting Roman Catholics"* he ever met. Tavener was deeply impressed by the spirituality and scholarship of the Carmelite, whom he credited with planting in him an intense desire to express metaphysical concepts by musical means. Through Malachy's influence, John Tavener came to regard music as a form of prayer. As a young man Tavener would regularly visit Aylesford Priory and Allington Castle, recalling that the walls of the latter were littered with notes encouraging artists and musicians to maintain 'the medieval spirit in art'. Tavener met with the Sufi, Anglican and Methodist friends that Malachy invited to Allington, and the Carmelite introduced him to Metropolitan Anthony Bloom, a meeting that nurtured the composer's attraction to the Orthodox Church, which he eventually joined. John Tavener was struck by the dramatic nature of Malachy's funeral, with the liturgy interspersed by torrential rain. Tavener later recalled that the opening section of a musical requiem entered his mind during the funeral, and the following sections unfolded during the drive home to London. This was the first of several instances of works coming to Tavener 'fully born', and he regarded it as a parting gift from the deceased. He wrote: *"The music has for me a deeply personal connection with Father Malachy, hence the use of the Latin singular throughout."* Tavener wrote the composition very quickly, and often came to Allington Castle to share with the Carmelites his thoughts on the work in progress. The *Little Requiem for Father Malachy Lynch* was first performed only two months later at the Southern Cathedral Festival, and in 1973 was performed at the Queen Elizabeth Hall in London's Southbank Centre. The *Little Requiem* was John Tavener's last respects to his wise mentor.

132

Sir John Tavener credited Father Malachy Lynch with nurturing his spiritual interests. By the time of his death in 2013, Tavener's extensive output of religious works had made him one of Britain's best known and loved composers.

After Malachy's death, some aspects of life at Aylesford changed. Apart from the pottery, many of the other projects there came to an end; a gradual decrease in the number of friars meant that the focus of their energies was put on supporting spirituality and visiting pilgrimage groups.

Pilgrims arriving at The Friars by boat in September 1975.

For a while after Malachy's death the 'Spanish Sisters' continued to help with catering and housekeeping, but their departure to work in Mozambique, where the need was greater, was felt as a great loss. Key aspects of the day-to-day running of the place were put into the hands of lay people, working in collaboration with the friar community.

133

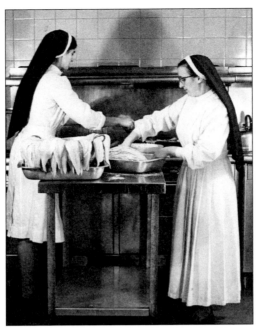

Sister Archimera (left) and Sister Lucy, Carmelite Sisters of the Sacred Heart
(Spanish Sisters) preparing fish for Friday lunch at Aylesford.

Arguably Malachy's memory has best been expressed by the fidelity the Carmelite community has showed to much of his sense of spirituality. Malachy's desire that The Friars should be a place of welcome and beauty has inspired efforts to continue enhancing the site. In the early years of the Twenty-First Century, flood defences were put in place thanks to a government bursary, and heritage grants enabled the renovation of the Gatehouse and North Barn.

In 2011 a Peace Garden was planted in the
driveway leading to the Gatehouse at The Friars.

134

The North Barn, renovated in 2005, is dedicated to Saint Edith Stein. A statue of her carved in wood by Geoff Lucas is an example of how Aylesford Priory continues to promote the arts as a means of connecting with the spiritual.

After Malachy's death, Allington Castle continued to flourish as a pastoral centre for schools and as an 'Open Door'. Sadly, however, with resources for the Carmelites becoming ever more stretched, the Castle was sold in 1995. It did invaluable work, and is remembered with great affection by the then young people who attended courses.

It is now over forty years since Father Malachy died, and his memory is still strong, not only at Aylesford and among Carmelites, but across the Catholic community in Britain. How can we both respect that memory, and also cast our nets into the deep, into the future?

Pilgrims gathered in front of the Main Shrine at Aylesford in 2007.

135

*Thousands of pilgrims came to Aylesford for the visit of
the relics of St. Thérèse of Lisieux in 2009.*

Part of Malachy's genius was to be able to read the signs of the times, and be in tune with the spiritual needs of the people. What he would make of Aylesford today would be fascinating to know, and how he would evangelise. These are challenging questions, but crucial if we would be creative and be able to build on the foundations that Malachy laid. The medieval buildings, the Shrine, the works of art, the beauty of nature, all create a sacred space. With no gates to be a barrier, Aylesford Priory is an 'Open Door' welcoming people of faith and those searching. Serving people's needs, offering hospitality, all of these make for a sense of welcome.

Carmelite friars at the front entrance of Aylesford Priory in 2007.

136

While much of Malachy's thought was tinged by a romantic vision of a medieval world restored, what really mattered was that he gave people time, and helped them feel as if they were accepted. In a bewildering world, respectful listening is invaluable, as it enables and heals. In an age when faith can have its ambiguities, it is important that the message of a merciful, healing God is proclaimed, and that the truth is not presented as an ideology but rather as a showing of the face of God.

Then Prior of Aylesford, Fr. Francis Kemsley, O.Carm., with the Prior General of the Carmelite Order, Fr. Fernando Millán Romeral, O.Carm., at Aylesford Priory during the 2008 Provincial Chapter of the British Province of Carmelites. The plaque, marking the return of the relics of Saint Simon Stock to Aylesford in 1951, 700 years after his reputed vision of Our Lady, translates: "The Flower of Carmel cut back now blossoms more vigorously".

137

I would hope that those who love Aylesford will help it remain in the future a beacon of hope, a light that guides and welcomes. The buildings took hard work and generosity to build; now it's their use and the creativity of the Carmelite Family. The buildings are now the context for people to enable hope and healing for our fragmented world. As ever, courage will be needed, but taking risks is a sign of trusting in the providence of God, and a willingness to be surprised as to where God will take us. Respecting Malachy's memory is not about copying the past, but risking the future, and living deep trust in God.

Bust of Malachy by Jaroslav Krechler in the Prior's Hall at The Friars.

138

Further Reading

Aylesford Priory ("The Friars")

- Edwina Fielding & Malachy Lynch, *Courage to Build Anew: The Story of the Rebuilding of The Friars, Aylesford, taken from the Newsletters of Father Malachy Lynch*, (London: Burns & Oates, 1968, Second edition 1989).

- Malachy Lynch, *Courage to Build Anew: The Pilgrim's Newsletters in full by Father Malachy Lynch, O.Carm.*, (Maidstone: The British Legion Press, 1975).

- *Return of the Whitefriars*, (Faversham: Carmelite Press, 1974).

- Wilfrid McGreal, O.Carm., *Aylesford – Pilgrim Guide*, (Norwich: The Canterbury Press, 1998).

- Wilfrid McGreal, *The History of The Friars, Aylesford*, (Norwich: Jarrold Publishing, 1998).

- James H. Sephton, *The Friars, Aylesford*, (Aylesford: James H. Sephton, 1999).

- *The Friars, Aylesford*, (Norwich: Jarrold Publishing, 2006).

Carmelite Spirituality

- John Welch, O.Carm., *The Carmelite Way: An Ancient Path for Today's Pilgrim*, (Leominster: Gracewing, 1996).

- Wilfrid McGreal, O.Carm., *At The Fountain of Elijah: The Carmelite Tradition*, Traditions of Christian Spirituality Series, (London: Darton, Longman & Todd, 1999).

- Johan Bergström-Allen, T.O.C., *Climbing the Mountain: The Carmelite Journey*, (Faversham & Rome: Saint Albert's Press & Edizioni Carmelitane, 2010, Second edition 2014).

The Lynch Brothers

- Wilfrid McGreal, O.Carm., *Friar Beyond The Pale: A Biography of Carmelite Friar Fr. Elias Lynch (1897-1967)*, (Faversham: Saint Albert's Press, 2007).

139

The Carmelite Family

The Carmelite Order is one of the ancient religious orders of the Roman Catholic Church. Known officially as the *Brothers of the Blessed Virgin Mary of Mount Carmel*, the Order developed from a group of hermits in thirteenth-century Israel-Palestine; priests and lay people living a contemplative life modelled on the prophet Elijah and the Virgin Mary. By the year 1214 the Carmelites had received a *Way of Life* from Saint Albert, the Latin Patriarch of Jerusalem.

Carmelites first came to Britain in 1242. The hermits became an order of mendicant friars following a General Chapter held in Aylesford, Kent, in 1247. Nuns, and lay men and women have always played a major part in the life of the Order, and have had formal participation since 1452. Over centuries of development and reform, the Carmelites have continued their distinctive mission of living 'in allegiance to Jesus Christ', by forming praying communities at the service of all God's people. The heart of the Carmelite vocation is contemplation, that is, openness to and friendship with God, pondering God's will in our lives.

Like the spirituality of all the major religious orders (Benedictines, Franciscans, Jesuits, etc.), Carmelite spirituality is a distinct preaching of the one Christian message. Carmelites blend a life of deep prayer with active service of those around them, and this apostolate takes many different forms depending on the time and the place Carmelites find themselves in.

Over the centuries 'Carmel' has produced some of the greatest Christian thinkers, mystics, and philosophers, such as Teresa of Jesus (of Avila), John of the Cross, and Thérèse of Lisieux (three Carmelite 'Doctors of the Church'). In the twentieth century, the Carmelite Family bore witness to the Gospel in the martyrdoms of Isidore Bakanja, Titus Brandsma, and Edith Stein.

England boasted the largest Carmelite Province in the Order until its suppression at the Reformation. The British Province was re-established under the patronage of Our Lady of the Assumption in the twentieth century. There are communities of friars, sisters and lay Carmelites across England, Scotland, and Wales. Similar communities exist in Ireland, and throughout the world. The international Order of Discalced (Teresian) Carmelite friars, nuns, and laity is also present in Britain and Ireland.

140

Members of the Carmelite and Discalced Carmelite Orders work, live, and pray together to make up the wider 'Carmelite Family', which seeks the face of the Living God in parishes, retreat centres, prisons, university and hospital chaplaincies, workplaces, schools, publishing, research, justice and peace work, counselling, and through many other forms of ministry and presence.

Website of the British Province of Carmelites

www.carmelite.org

The Carmelite Institute of Britain & Ireland (CIBI)

CIBI was established in 2005 to diffuse the charism, heritage and spirituality of 'Carmel' through part-time distance-learning courses in Carmelite Studies at introductory and more advanced levels.

The Institute's scholarly but accessible programmes are open to members of the Carmelite Family and anyone interested in the field of Carmelite Studies.

Through its interdisciplinary courses and activities, the Institute offers an opportunity to learn about Carmelite life in its many forms, as well as a means to grow intellectually, spiritually and professionally.

CIBI's programmes – ranging from an *Adult Education Diploma* to postgraduates courses in Carmelite Studies – are accredited by institutions of Higher Education, giving professional qualifications to those students who opt to submit assessments.

Thanks to the founders and sponsors of the Institute – a joint initiative of the Carmelite and Discalced Carmelite Orders in Britain and Ireland – programmes are made available to students at very reasonable rates, with a certain number of bursaries awarded to deserving individuals.

Though based in Britain and Ireland, CIBI enjoys close links with study institutes, libraries and heritage projects around the world, and welcomes student applications from any country.

For further information and a prospectus, please contact:

The Carmelite Institute of Britain & Ireland
Gort Muire Carmelite Centre, Ballinteer, Dublin 16, Ireland
☎ +353 (0)1 298 7706
E-mail: admin@cibi.ie
www.cibi.ie